*From Our Father's Heart ... To You*
**ISBN: 0-9657268-2-7**

*a devotional*
*by*
Jim and Merry Corbett

Words and Exhortations
*inspired by*
*our*
Father in Heaven

"From Our Father's Heart ... To You"
ISBN 0 - 9657268-2-7

is a companion book
to
"A White Stone"
ISBN 0 - 9657268-0-0
and
"A White Stone Workbook"
ISBN 0 - 9657268-1-9

Published and distributed
by
COMMUNITY SERVICES NETWORK
P.O. BOX 1116
BROOKFIELD, WISCONSIN 53008-1116

Cover Design by Ada Arneson

Printed in U.S.A.
ISBN: 0-9657268-2-7

Acknowledgments
To:
**Father God,**
for Your undying love and merciful heart.
May You be glorified as we turn to You.

*Dr. Kathy Bojanowski,*
*for your valuable assistance in*
*applying Biblical verses to each Father's Heart Message.*

*Ron Plender,*
*for your faith, encouragement and*
*servanthood in the preparation, editing and publishing*
*of this effort.*
*You are a valuable friend.*

*Mack and Debbie Karnes,*
*for your continued love and support.*
*We are blessed to have friends like you.*

*Marianne Schulz,*
*for all your encouragement.*
*Your commitment to Jesus continues*
*to "spur" us on.*

## From The Authors

We are not prophets. Although some of the material contained in the following pages is often categorized as prophetic, we do not ever claim to be prophets. If there is a need for you to classify this work, let it suffice to say that we are watchmen, heralding what we believe to be the heart of our Father - watchmen with an urgent message of repentance and the need to pursue holiness.

We are also ambassadors - ambassadors of Jesus Christ, as all of you are if you have given your life to Him fully. We believe that the entire Word of God (especially 2 Corinthians 5:18-20) tells us that we are all greatly loved children of our heavenly Father; and therefore, ambassadors and ministers of reconciliation to this world for Him. Each of us, then, is first and foremost a child of God with that mission. *That is what we are, all else is what we do.*

With that in mind, Merry and I would like to present the following words, commentaries and simple encouragements that were inspired by the Lord in times of prayer and fellowship with Him. We realize that there is a fine line between something *inspired by* and something claimed to be the words *of* God, especially when they are stated in the first person as if they were from the Lord directly - which is how some of these are written. You, the reader, will be asked to make that determination through prayer.

Please prayerfully take all that is contained in this effort back to the Lord and His Word, so that He might confirm its validity. You then have a choice as to what you'll do with the contents of the book. We strongly recommend, however, that you base any of life's decisions solely on the written Word of God and wise counsel. All other resources, including this one, should be supplementary and used only if in line with His Word - and then only as He leads you after proper study, prayer and research.

As His ambassadors and watchmen, we desire that you see our Father's heart. May you be refreshed, exhorted to draw close to Him and choose to serve Him with new vigor as He reveals Himself to you through His Holy Spirit. If this effort has a small part in doing that, we will be greatly blessed and encouraged to continue to do what we do *with* Him, while remaining who we are *in* Him.

In His Steps,

Jim and Merry Corbett

## How To Use This Book

It is our hope that this book breaks your heart. Our prayer is that you, the reader, sense the love and compassion that our Father God has for you. We also pray that you will see His intense commitment to His Word to do everything possible to draw each of us to true repentance and dedication to Him in these last hours - that we might be a pure and holy bride.

This book is designed as part of a "Heart Revival Kit," which includes the novel "A White Stone" and "A White Stone Workbook." Although we would recommend that you read those books before you use this devotional (because of references contained in them,) it is not absolutely necessary. The three together, however, do comprise a continual resource that allows the Holy Spirit to expose your true motives for what you do. Allow Him to lead you back to His Word as you are challenged by His loving presence while you wait on Him.

Please introduce yourself to the contents contained herein as you would to a new friend. Take the time to become familiar with its pages at random, that it might be revealed how the book could serve you. In subsequent visits, travel back to your Father to learn more of Him and His desires as you read. Do not travel to too many places in one visit, but visit often and let the Holy Spirit direct your times together. Allow the Lord over the years, as you open its (hopefully by then) well-worn pages, to reveal Himself to you to the point of true intimacy.

Remember, your Father in heaven is not angry with

you, but loves you very much. Even the strongest language with the most intense words comes from a heart of compassion. He is always deep in love with His children, and continually desirous of moving them to a place of safety nearer to Himself. It is always for our good that His warnings and exhortations come to us, no matter what form they take. Our obedience to His call determines how well we will be able to hear Him in the future. If the contents of this book confirm what the Lord is saying to your heart, do not delay in responding to the Holy Spirit's call. Do what it takes to draw close to your loving Father.

Jim

Final note:

When Merry and I began writing the commentaries for the "Father's Hearts," we prayerfully selected them "at random." At first glance, some of them seem unrelated to either the "Father's Heart" or the Bible Correlations.

Upon closer scrutiny, you will find that they open up an additional direction for you to pursue in prayer. Our intent is to stimulate deeper thought and prayerful waiting, so that God can bring revival to your heart. What may seem unrelated at first, you will find to be very much in accord with an overall pursuit of a deeper revelation of our Lord and His purposes.

# CONTENTS

# Let's Begin

**God's plan is always to bring us back to Himself.**

*"....God does not take away life; instead, He devises ways so that a banished person may not remain estranged from Him."*
2 Samuel 14:14

.......................................................................................

*"So God created man in His own image, in the image of God He created him; male and female He created them."*
Gen. 1:27

God created man and woman to have fellowship with Himself. Throughout the whole Bible, God is impressing upon His people that He is God, and we are to be His people. When the first man and woman fell away from God through disobedience, they rejected the idea of this total need and submission. This same heritage, a rebellious nature that wants to feel and act on its own, has been passed down to each of us. We feel that we can get along without God controlling our lives.

God has, however, created a plan that allows each of us to choose whether or not we want to be back in that original relationship with Him. Each of us can say "yes" to Him by accepting Jesus Christ as <u>Lord of our life</u>, reinstating Him as our God, and being reconciled to Him in truth.

When we decide to make Jesus our Lord, a covenant which God has established to change our nature to one that desires to serve Him is put into effect. We become new creatures, reborn to love being in service to God; and He, in turn, commits Himself to us.

With this wonderful, miraculous provision in mind, we begin to look at :

## THE COVENANT, OR CONTRACT, WITH GOD

Most of us have somehow been led to believe that the plan of God was finished soon after He created Adam and Eve. Few of us consider that we may be, and most likely are, simply the next creation of millions of future creations planned by God. We limit our understanding of God by attempting to put Him in our very small "understanding box," and then wonder why it seems impossible to understand Him as all that He claims to be as our God.

In this segment of the eternal history of creation (which we see in the Bible and of which we are a part,) we, in our carnal thinking, generally assume that there must have been some kind of emergency meeting of the Trinity to see how God could get out of this great, unforeseen dilemma that had come about because of the fall in the Garden of Eden. Nothing could be further from the truth. As of this moment, we are all "playing out" the continual, unfolding plan for this stage of mankind's existence - about to enter into the next stage in God's plan when all things are fulfilled, whenever He chooses to reveal it to us.

## The beginning as we know it

The only other creation that we are allowed knowledge of is the creation and fall of the beings that the Bible calls angels. This creation is usually not associated with the overall plan for mankind; but their fall, and subsequent ejection from heaven, formed the demonic forces that continually play a part in the working out of the salvation of each of us at this present time. What is interesting to note with this scenario, is that they did not have a chance for redemption after they committed the same rebellion that was to occur in God's next creation. Their rebellion was final, and had final consequences.

## Enter Mankind

( Read Genesis 1:1 - 3:24 )

God <u>continued</u> our salvation process when He formed Adam and placed His breath within him. The being that would eventually rebel against its Creator in an attempt to function independently from Him, was given life - God's Life. Mankind was designated "good" in the eyes of God; the perfect companion to Him as seen through the corridors of time to a time when all things would be in order, probably sometime in our near future. Formed perfectly, and in complete fellowship as planned, God loved and cared for His creation.

In the beginning, God was the complete source for all that His child needed, and that same child was totally fulfilled by his Lord and Master. He owned all that could ever be needed or wanted as part of the provisional promise of his Master's relationship.

## But it wasn't enough

The stage for the kind of future intimacy that God desired was set when the law was established. If mankind had chosen to remain obedient to God in every way, there would have been no need for what was about to unfold for generations to come. But as God knew all along, disobedience was inevitable and rebellion was about to occur. In choosing to be independent of the desires of God, mankind chose to leave the protective covering of the absolutes of his Lord and join in with the original rebellion, making himself an ally with his new master.

This choice changed the nature of all mankind, for all mankind, at the time, had made the choice. In essence, the choice was really the manifestation of the desire to be like God, and to come out from under His authority. It was the same decision that the angels had previously made, but now they were being used as part of the working out of the redemption of mankind.

Mankind decided to function independently from God, calling on Him when needed; but not desiring to be in total submission to Him. The chief of the fallen angels (Satan) was even then in the process of playing into the hands of God, and the rebellion that he initiated was used for his own eventual defeat.

## God used covenants
## to prepare the way for Jesus.

God's intended system of choosing between good and evil having been established, it allowed all subsequent generations the freedom to make the choice of whom they would willingly serve. Mankind, however, was at a distinct disadvantage. The master, or father, that Adam and Eve chose was a hard taskmaster, requiring total allegiance. He was at war with God Himself, and demanded that his children violate every principle that the Creator had established. Using every means that appealed to the now separated man - lust, pride, envy, murder, and many more - an attempt to distance the creation from his Creator was in full force. While his pawns remained in the false comfort of thinking that they were free to "do their own thing," they were, in reality, fully serving their father the devil, <u>to be individually separated from God for eternity</u>. ( John 8: 42 - 47 ) The creation, apart from its Creator, was on a downward spiral, hopeless to break away from the grip of its master.

During this time, however, God would find people who loved Him; people He could trust who would make alliances or covenants with Him to carry on the hope of the coming salvation and release mankind from this death grip. Abraham, Noah, David, the prophets - all those obedient to His Word - became vessels to carry His life. It was God hovering over His Word to perform it, using those who were willing to work with Him to warn those who wouldn't or couldn't hear.

When men and women had sufficiently proven that they had no good within themselves, (the fruit of their depravity being clear for all future generations to see;) many cried out to God to deliver them from the bondage that had been created by generations of separation. The culmination of four thousand years of failing God was a time of silence in the heavenlies. For four hundred years, a wailing to God for deliverance was common, only to go unanswered until true heart seeking came about through the deep awareness of their need and helplessness without a Savior.

## The Final Covenant

All previous contracts with God were doomed to eventual failure because of the fallen nature of  man. Man simply couldn't keep them. Obedience to God brought God's provision. Those that were obedient soon prospered. As soon as he was blessed with God's presence and prospered, man soon forgot *why* his life was in order and turned away from the obedience that brought the blessing in the first place. God, on the other hand, continually kept His part of every contract until it was broken. When man broke his promise, God then searched until someone else could be trusted to make another agreement. Agreement after agreement was made and broken by man until God showed a way that would finally work. He would make a covenant with Himself.

## Our Covenant Keeper

The Spirit of Jesus, as God, was breathed into Adam and Eve. That pure Spirit was kept unblemished through direct lineage until it manifested itself in the man, Jesus, Who walked among His creation. Born of woman, fathered by the Holy Spirit  Himself and entrusted legally to the bloodline of Adam through Joseph, Jesus was the perfect provision for all of mankind.

Jesus' flawless keeping of all of the Law of God as man, fulfilled man's original requirement to be obedient. His three years of untarnished submission to God, while filled with the Holy Spirit, gave us a pattern for our lives when we too would have God's Spirit within us, after the work of the cross had been accomplished. The death of the man, Jesus, killed the flesh, the part that could not serve God; while the resurrection overcame death forever. *As God, Jesus made a covenant with God that would never be broken again. He, as God, would keep it and as man, entered into that same agreement for each of us.*

## The stage was set for the fulfillment of all things.

You and I have the very distinct privilege of living in the era of the culmination of all things as we know them. Only the final events of the biblical calendar need to take place in order to fulfill all things. No other generation has had the position of being able to see history as it has already unfolded, while  at the same time had enough insight (because of biblical revelation,) to see how the future will unfold. Events that were written with early  technological parameters are easily explainable for us today because of the society in which  we live and the technology available.  We can accurately predict much of what and how the end will occur, simply by applying  today's technology and political patterns to the foretold biblical events. All is in place and poised to unfold in obedience to the command of our God. He will determine when  all things are in order and everything is fulfilled. After those final events occur in our near future, mankind will enter into the one thousand years of walking with Jesus, God Himself, just as in the Garden of Eden. The full, biblical life circle will be completed and our originally intended positions with God will be in operation for all eternity.

It is with this scenario in mind that these pages are presented. If we are really living in the last minutes of the biblical calendar, where all things must be fulfilled, (the New World Order coming into being, the Antichrist almost at the door with his mark for each person that accepts it; and the breakdown of society as we know it,) what should our position be? Should it not be one of submitting fully to God as He has intended from the beginning? Should we not discern the times and seasons in which we live and realize that our sole purpose for breathing is to do the will of the One Who has created us? Is it not our portion, when we see all things being fulfilled in the daily news, to shake off the things that distract us, and live like Jesus did in His generation, warning them of the times in which they lived? I think so.

I believe that God is calling His endtime generation (you and I) to a walk of holiness and complete devotion to Him. He is clearly desiring that those whom He has called to Himself act like His Son, Jesus, did to the world. I am convinced that He is not angry with us; but at the same time, He is very sincere in His exhortations for us to receive and live out His salvation plan for the world to see. We are to be a holy people, full of the true Spirit of God through Jesus. We are to be empowered with love, dead to anything of the world and walking in the restored, full, unbroken fellowship with God.

May you choose to become more and more like His Son, Jesus, and submit to the desires of God. It is our hope that this effort will help you draw close and recognize a call of love "From Our Father's Heart ... To You."

# RECOGNITION

Please note. A few of the writings in this book have been presented in some fashion before, such as in our monthly ministry newsletter which is distributed locally. There are some, however, that have been published on a wider scale, such as those that were written in "A White Stone" and its companion workbook.

There are also writings that have been included by permission in the highly recommended book, "The Last Call" ( ISBN 0-9633026 ) by R.C. Schaffter; Published and Distributed by The Clarion Call, P.O. Box 335, Lannon Wisconsin 53046. Note that there are some minor modifications and author's brackets that differ from our publication. All differences have been handled prayerfully and permission was given to make minor modifications when necessary. The alterations in no way compromise the spirit, intent or integrity of the writings.

The following compilation is a consolidation of all of the above material, but also includes many writings that have never been published before. It is now published because of the leading of our Lord and numerous requests to do so. Our prayer is that you use these writings in conjunction with the written Word as part of your continuing pursuit to know God better.

## Section A

These first "Father's Hearts" correspond to the thirty-one chapters in the companion book "A White Stone." After the novel was written, the Lord impressed on me to place some of them at the beginning of each chapter. This sent me back to prayer because there were over eighty-five messages and only thirty-one chapters.

In a little while, it seemed that He was asking me to lay them all out on the living room floor. Then, He would almost "light them up" and give me a chapter number at the same time. I placed all of them at the beginning of each chapter without reading them. When I was finished and saw how each placement corresponded so completely with the text of the chapter, my heart was once more in awe of our God.

## FROM OUR FATHER'S HEART (A1)
### From Chapter 1 of "A White Stone"

*How many people have seen My Son*
*in your life?*
*How many have chosen*
*to serve Me through My Son*
*because they have seen Him in you?*
*How many have turned from their ways*
*to My ways*
*because of your ways?*
*Does your neighbor know*
*that you are My tabernacle?*
*Does your enemy know*
*that you are told*
*to lay your life down for him and have agreed to do so?*
*Do you know that I love the abortionist,*
*the pornographer,*
*the homosexual?*
*Do you know that I have sent you to them*
*that they might see My Son through you,*
*that they might accept Him?*
*Do you have the eternity*
*of your every contact in mind*
*when you address them?*
*If not, why not?*

## Bible Correlations

Matt. 10:16,19 amp.;   Matt. 25:35-40;
Luke 14:23 amp;   2 Cor. 5:17

Do these questions make you say, "ouch?" In addition to "ouch," they make me say "only by your grace, Lord." I know all these things in my head, but are they really in my heart?

In spite of our human failures, I believe that God allows His Son to be seen in us as it suits His purposes. Haven't you found that someone saw Jesus in you even when you were unaware of being observed?

Take courage.   Your Lord is taking you through the process of going from glory to glory. He chooses to make you part of His plan of love and salvation to others, knowing that you haven't "arrived," yet. (Be fearful of the time when you think that you just might  have it all together!)

## FROM OUR FATHER'S HEART (A2)
### From Chapter 2 of "A White Stone"

Do not worry,
for I have My hand on you.
You shall not lack.
Do not look to the things that are said by man.
My hand directs the stars.
My voice commands the rivers to flow.
They would stop if I desired it.
My desire is for you to serve Me.
Nothing will stop that.
Draw close.
I notice the terrors of Satan
that bluff
and talk as if they know what they are saying.
They do not know what I have in store
other than what I have told them.
You shall go forth, for I am your God -
not the God that can be changed by the whims of people,
but the God that is moved by faith in Me,
being able to perform what I promise.
Have I not promised you?
When will you realize the magnitude of My power?
When will you begin to truly trust Me?
Seek Me for Me; not for what I can do for you,
but for Who I am as God.
You have no idea what I have in store for you,
but I am excited by what I see.
I am pleased by My people that have said "yes."
When I am pleased,
all creation knows that I am God.

## Bible Correlations

*Ps. 34:8-10;   Isa. 40:21-31;   Isa. 46:10-11;*
*John 6:37 amp;   Heb. 11:3&6*

When will we finally settle it in our hearts that God is in control, even when we think that we are? Nothing gets past Him. Anything that we experience, He has allowed into our lives. We need to trust His purposes and His reasons, whether or not we know and understand what they are. Our place is to simply know that everything is used by Him to draw us to Him. Everything that happens is His work in us; forming a heart that trusts and willingly serves Him.

The next time you face any adversity, remind yourself that the Lord knows all about it. Wait on Him to find out what part, if any, you play in the solution before you do anything. Sometimes, you need do nothing to remove yourself from the situation because He is making internal changes in you. Remain in the fire and allow Him to refine you into useable gold.

# FROM OUR FATHER'S HEART (A3)
## From Chapter 3 of "A White Stone"

As the world grows darker,
My people
will shine brighter because of the love they have for Me,
each other and their enemies.
This love has already been established in the heavenlies,
and is about to be poured out in its fullness
upon My people.
Holy alliances will be made one with another.
Kinsman friendships will be established
that cannot be intruded upon by the vile jestings
and coarse intrusions
that are part of those who do not know Me.
I call you to separate yourselves,
but in that separation,
I am also calling you, My children,
to come together.
Some of you know the bond of adversity,
some know the bond of fleshly desire and adoration,
some know the safety of a kindred spirit;
but no one has known the heavenly bond
of the holy alliance that will knit My bride together
for My work to be done
and for Me to pour My love upon them.
Establish it in your hearts now.
Those I call to Myself will know Me, and each other,
with the love My Father and I have had
from the beginning.

Make no provision for the flesh
in any relationships I bring your way.
In My way, there's safety,
power,
freedom
and love.

Bible Correlations

Amos 3:3;   John 13:34-35;   John 17 :22-23

Isn't  it interesting to watch God establish relationships? If
you haven't given it much thought, just know that this is one more
area that works out best when put in His hands. He has a purpose
for every relationship, and He has reasons for not wanting others
established.

When I  go about the business of establishing any relationship on my own, more than likely for selfish reasons, I should  not
be surprised when it doesn't work  out. If God, however, brings
someone into my life and it is not  working, more than likely my
heart is not right.  I want my way, my desires, not His.

Periodically, I find myself wanting to befriend someone,
but it just doesn't  fall together. It is then that I need to remind

myself that if it is God-ordained, He will bring that friendship into existence. He will make all of the necessary adjustments, heart modifications and motive refinements to allow all things to fall in line. He will orchestrate and finalize any other aspects of personality to smooth out the rough spots that stand in the way. He sees the total picture. He knows the beginning and the end, the reasons and the consequences. We don't.

In the coming seasons, it will become increasingly important that God is really in charge. We will need to be able to trust the people within our sphere of friendships. There will be times that lives will depend on the ability to do so. At that time, who would you like to have established the relationships in your life?

## FROM OUR FATHER'S HEART (A4)
### From Chapter 4 of "A White Stone"

I call you to holiness,
but you are too busy to spend time with Me.
I call you to a crucified life,
but you cannot die to yourself.
I call you to present My Son
to those who are dead that they might receive His life, but you
curse them in My presence.
Can you not see how cold you really are?
Can you not see how far you've strayed
from My purposes for your life?
Who are you saving by your actions?
What are the purposes of your comings and goings? Whose
agenda are you following, and what is its end?
Wake up.
The harvest is ripe and the workers are few.
Pray to the Lord of the harvest.
What are His purposes?
What is His agenda?
Pray for wisdom that you might see with His eyes
and move with His heart.
The time is short and much is to be done.

## Bible Correlations

Isa. 30:15-18;  Amos 6:1;  Amos 6:5-7;
John 4:34-38;  Rom. 13:10-14;  2 Cor. 4:7

Do we live for God, or for ourselves? It is really a very important question that each of us must ask ourselves if we call ourselves His, and call Him Lord. The truthful answer will be the basis for every decision that we make. Will we spend time in God's presence to receive His directions, submit to His plans and become like His Son, or will we choose our own way? Going our own way satisfies our flesh, even if we do good deeds and help just causes.

Choosing God's will and submitting to His ways is not easy if we do not take the time to know Him. Knowing Him will allow us to love Him. Loving Him will allow us to submit fully. It makes sense that when we love someone, we will naturally desire to fulfill their wishes. We will more readily try to please someone that we know, deep in our spirit, loves us unconditionally. Wouldn't it be wonderful if every thought and action of ours came out of a heart of love for God, rather than from a sense of duty?

God's intent is for us to first love Him, and then love people enough to spend our lives for them, so that they will see Who Jesus really is. What is your intent for living? What is your purpose for getting up each morning? Is it the same as God's? If not, why not?

## FROM OUR FATHER'S HEART (A5)
### From Chapter 5 of "A White Stone"

"In the Name of the Lord," you say.
You go about your business doing your works
and call them Mine.
How can what you do be truly Mine
if you don't spend enough time with Me
to hear Me, to search My heart, to find My ways,
to know Me?
I am not in your feasts.
I am not in your programs.
I am not in your fellowships.
A time is coming
when those who think they hear My voice
will see and understand
who they have really been listening to.
It is not Me.
All the works of the flesh will wash away as so much grime.
I will not complete what I did not initiate.
Stop praying for things.
Stop working for men and their desires.
Begin praying to search Me out.
I can be found.
I desire to be found.
Those who choose to know Me are wise.
Those who come to Me
will walk the straight, safe path.
My ways are sure.
My time is well spent for those who have heard Me.

## Bible Correlations

Isa. 1:10-20;
Isa. 29:13-14;   Jer. 29:12-14;   Matt. 6:33

Not all of the good things that we do are God-ordained things. When we uncomplicate our lives by spending time with God and see that most of what we are involved in has little to do with His plans for us, He begins to set us free. Busy work, even good work that does not allow us time to develop an intimacy with Him, is not of Him.

When we seek to know God, He will reveal Himself and impart Himself to us. We will begin to know His heart and what is most important to Him. He will show areas where our participation is requested and when it is not. He will show us when to say "no" and when to move in His power. What is important to Him will become important to us. The rest will fall pale and will be of little significance, even those things that formerly meant so much to us.

It is time to ask our Lord to teach us to let go of the things of this world by understanding more clearly what He would hang on to. The closer we get to Him, the easier it is to see what hinders us from getting to know Him better. As we experience the vast riches of knowing Him, our hands will no longer cling to the puny things of this world, but will open wide in submission. Try it, you'll like it.

## FROM OUR FATHER'S HEART (A6)
### From Chapter 6 of "A White Stone"

Your carnal mind cannot begin to understand
what I have planned for you.
I call you My children, that You can understand.
When My glory is manifested,
My Word says that you will be as I am.
(1 John 3:2)
If you could only believe.
If you would only come close enough
that I might express Myself to you.
Your eyes are big towards what is happening around you.
In your disloyalty, the world is powerful.
In your obedience,
you can see a little more of My perspective.
There is nothing too hard for Me.
There is nothing to fear
if you choose intimacy with Me over activity in the flesh.
My plans for you - who you are now
and what you shall become -
do not depend on the world and its ways.
They are not changed by loud voices.
Understand I do not change.
I do not waver.
I do not fail.
My Word is true and at work even now in the din of life.
To see My purposes, you must turn to Me.
I don't mean for you to pray about things;
I ask you to come to be changed.
I am not interested in what you do
as much as I am interested in who you are becoming.

*How can old things pass away*
*if you remain in them?*
*You are no longer part of this world.*
*Separate yourself from it,*
*for it is soon passing away.*
*Only My Word, My ways, will remain.*
*Come to Me now.*
*I love you.*

Bible Correlations

Ps. 119:89;  Jer. 32:17;  Mal. 3:6;
Luke 1:37;  Jas. 1:2-3

There comes a time in your walk with  the Lord  when you simply take a leap of faith and choose to believe that He is Who He says He is, that His Word is true and at work in you; and that He will complete the work He started in you.

You can't change yourself; only  God  can change you. The world and its ways of bringing about change will only disappoint.  Why then, do we continue to try it the world's way? Could it be that it's the voice that speaks the loudest? The voice that has our attention? The voice that is all too familiar?

God  so longs to embrace us and teach us to dwell in His realm. He never disappoints once we understand the truth. All that He asks is that we come to Him, so that He can do in us what no one else can - make us whole.

## FROM OUR FATHER'S HEART (A7)
### From Chapter 7 of "A White Stone"

From My perspective,
some of you are acting no differently
than the world that is perishing.
You are using its methods to change its unchangeable heart.
Why would you think that true,
lasting change can be accomplished by the ways of man?
Laws never change hearts,
for the heart is wicked.
When you move in the flesh, fleshly changes result.
I have never called you to pursue anything but Me.
When you do that,
we move in the spiritual realm to change hearts,
to save those who are perishing.
My Word shows how fallen man
is helpless to even see the need to repent and change his ways.
My Word shows
how My covenant is invoked when My Spirit
moves on the heart to come to repentance.
When that happens, eternal changes result.
That is My way.
You cannot see, however,
because you want changes your way
and you are ineffective
because I cannot be with you to empower you
because it is not My way.
It never will be.

*I have one purpose for you now that you are Mine.*
*It is the purpose that My Holy Spirit,*
*Who is now in you, has always had.*
*He has always proclaimed the beauty*
*of Jesus*
*to a world out of answers,*
*a world dying in its sin.*
*He has always moved*
*so that those who are perishing might see,*
*and come*
*and be saved.*
*Why are you not moving in that same direction?*
*All else that seems important is folly.*
*I am not in it.*
*Why would you be?*

Bible Correlations

Prov. 14:29;  Jer. 17:9;  Eze. 36:26-27 amp;
John 5:30b;  John 15:26-27;
2 Cor. 2:14-16

*Lasting change is spiritual. It is birthed in the spirit realm.*
*It is maintained in the spirit realm. Even when we know this, why*
*do we still try to employ fleshly ways to bring about a spiritual*

result? Could it be that the fleshly way is more convenient and appealing to us? Could it be that we don't even see when our methods are of the flesh? Oops!

How important it is to know God, to spend time in His presence. What could be better than spending time with the Lord in order to be able to distinguish spirit from flesh?

Our flesh is weak, for many other things capture our attention. How wonderful it is to know that it is not our flesh that maintains what God has begun in the spirit.

Maybe it is now time to thank God for His Spirit which He has placed in each and every believer. It might also be a good time to get to know His still, small voice, so that we will be able to avoid the pitfalls encountered when we attempt to move on our own, hearing our fleshly voice.

## FROM OUR FATHER'S HEART (A8)
### From Chapter 8 of "A White Stone"

My holding power
is much more powerful
than the sinning power of your flesh.
When will you grasp the reality
of what has been done on the cross for you?
Its work runs deeper than any force.
Its power is so much greater
than anything that may attempt to come against it.
When Jesus died,
all that hindered My presence
from becoming active and available in your life
was removed forever.
When He arose, death itself was defeated.
Think on that.
What that means for you
is the freedom to receive My life,
My eternal life,
and the wealth that comes to you
by My presence being with you in your life forever.
When hardship comes,
don't attempt to deal with it by your knowledge or ability.
Apply My life to it.
Wait for My presence to move.
Rest in Me.
See My work being done in all situations.
Be free by My Spirit
and you will have an abundance
no matter what the outward circumstances might appear to be.

## Bible Correlations

*Prov. 3:5-6;*
*Ps. 34:7 amp; Ps. 121; Jude 24,25*

At some point in my walk with the Lord, He enabled me to decide to simply trust Him to keep me, to change me to become more and more like Jesus, and to fully orchestrate my life. I believe a lot of it had to do with Him allowing me to see how ineffective I was in trying to do all of those things in my own strength. Many opportunities are still presented that remind me of my incredible need for God - something that I am thankful He will never allow me to forget.

It is not always easy, but continual waiting in the presence of God in prayer is the only way to life, peace and freedom.

## FROM OUR FATHER'S HEART (A9)
### From Chapter 9 of "A White Stone"

As My people go about their own version
of what My Word says,
I, the Lord God,
am used as a license for them to remain in their sin,
or
I am  left out completely.
Where in My Word does it say
that My people are to be political
or moral watchdogs?
Where in My Word does it say
that My people are to condemn the sinner?
Where in My Word does it say that My people
are to search out those things that give them comfort?
I have called My people to holiness.
I have called My people
to be set apart from all that resembles the world.
I sent My Son
that the dead may be given life.
All do not receive that life.
They choose to remain dead.
Your flurry of activities,
your agenda of issue involvement,
your moral judgment
and all of its associated activities
have not
and cannot
bring life to those who are dead.

I am not in your outcry against your world.
I am only in your outcry for mercy for your hardened heart.
Repent and turn now.
See your spiritual adultery.
See your hardened hearts.
See your dead, cold churches
and weep for them.
I have called you
to tell the blind of a way
that they might see My Son,
Jesus Christ.
Why do you insist on doing your own will
rather than submitting to Me
to have your heart changed
that they might see Jesus
in you?

Bible Correlations

Lev. 11:44-45;  John 17:17;  Acts 3:19;
2 Cor. 10:4a kjv;  Eph. 6:10-12 niv;
1 Pe. 2:9;  Rev. 3:1-2

There is only one interpretation of the Bible that's always accurate - it's God's interpretation. We can use the Word all we want to justify what we believe and how we act and still not be functioning in the truth. We can pick and choose scriptures until we are blue in the face, but all we need do is examine the life of Jesus, study the example He set and then do likewise. That is one of the reasons He came. We need to follow someone who walked in the truth.

If you look at Jesus' life, He exhibited pity and compassion for the unsaved, and reserved His harshest comments for those who should have known and functioned in the truth in the first place - the church. We have a tendency to do just the opposite, because that's what the flesh wants to do - stand up for its rights in the worldly arena and blast those who can't understand the truth yet.

How can we possibly reach the lost if their eyes and ears and hearts have not been touched by the Holy Spirit with the truth of the Gospel? The key is love, not finger pointing. The key is prayer, not just picketing. The key is Christ in us, the hope of glory; not just empty words with no holy lifestyle to back them up.

People need the Lord. They need to see Him in us.

# FROM OUR FATHER'S HEART (A10)
## *From Chapter 10 of "A White Stone"*

*If only you would learn to walk in the Spirit*
*and not in the flesh.*
*My will would be known to you daily,*
*but you miss out on many blessings I have for you.*
*I have not called you to a walk of life;*
*but death to your flesh.*
*Through that death comes life, My life for you.*
*Have I not called you to take up your cross daily*
*and to follow Me?*
*To do away with self and self-will?*
*Have I not called you for My purpose*
*and My purpose only?*
*I see My church*
*and I know the things that go on in My church.*
*Nothing is hidden from Me.*
*Everything exposed by the light becomes visible*
*for it is the light that makes everything visible.*
*(Ephesians 5:13-14; Numbers 32:23)*
*First love! First love!*
*I am calling you.*
*Look to your first love with Me.*
*Many of you make other things your first love.*
*I am a jealous God*
*and I will remove everything that comes between you and Me.*
*I love you too much to have us separated.*
*It is not to dishearten you*
*or discourage you in any way,*
*but so that you will really know the love I have for you.*

### Bible Correlations

Matt. 16:24;   Acts 2:42-47 niv;   Gal. 2:20;
Gal. 5:25;   Heb. 12:25-29;   Rev.2:4

In Isaiah 30:18liv, God says: "I will conquer you to bless you." In human terms, that makes no sense. "If I'm conquered, everything is taken from me. I'm worse off than before. I'll have to start over." Yes! That's the idea! Start over. So often what we consider life turns out to be death in God's eyes.

Once we discover that our own righteousness is filthy rags, we don't exactly know what to expect if we lay it all down; so we still cling to something with which we're familiar - our family, success, reputation, our own idea of what our walk with God should be. "I can't just lay it all down. What if it's all taken away? What then?"

Every once in awhile, I get into my "waiting for the other shoe to drop" mentality. "Let's see. God just required this of me. I wonder what else I'm going to have to lose or suffer?" Or, "Things have been going too good lately. This can't last much longer." Obviously, something is wrong with my perspective if I stack it up with what the Bible says about God and what adversity is meant to accomplish.

Somehow, in those moments of dread, I've lost God's perspective and a picture of who He really is. He is not waiting around for opportune moments to pull the rug out from under us. That's something man would do and probably delight in it. Don't equate God's thoughts and intents with man's. There is no correlation. He is desirous of an all-consuming relationship with us and it breaks His heart to see us embrace those things which stop that from coming about.

We, on the other hand, have only a dim view of what He sees and knows and is. Those other loves are all too present, convenient and familiar, obscuring our view of the things that would be the biggest blessings of all - the things that God considers important. After all, doesn't the Creator know what is best for His creation? He knows how His creation was designed to exist and live.

Let's stop trying to alter the blueprints, and seek God to know His plan for us. Each one of us was custom-designed by an all-wise God; and who would know better what we need and what would truly bless us than Him?

# FROM OUR FATHER'S HEART (A11)
## From Chapter 11 of "A White Stone"

*Healthy life comes from pure seed.*
*The purest seed has fallen willingly to the ground and died.*
*It is My Son,*
*Jesus.*
*I have raised Him up and glorified Him*
*for all eternity.*
*Should you not follow the example of My Son?*
*Why do you hang on to rotting seed*
*when I am the source of a life*
*that is untouchable by the death*
*and decay of this world?*
*Hold on to those things that bring true Life,*
*not those things that are perishing.*
*I have shown you the way, now walk in it.*
*Do not look to the left or to the right,*
*but only to Me*
*for I am with you.*
*You must trust Me and Me alone.*
*Your only safety is in the life of My Son,*
*Jesus.*
*That means a complete death to your way of doing things.*
*It will cost you everything.*
*But it is My way*
*for your best life.*

## Bible Correlations

Matt. 5:44 kjv;  Luke 18:18-30;  John. 12:24;
Rom. 12:1-2;  Phil. 2:8-11;  1 Ti 6:4-12;
Heb. 12:1-2;  1 Pe. 1:6-7

Our words have lost their effectiveness because of loose usage. Satan has purposefully made shades of gray through half-truths, traditions and flat-out lies. He doesn't want the concept of absolute truth to be fully understood. If he can nullify absolutes, he has succeeded in nullifying our effectiveness to represent the truth of Jesus. Holiness means sort of holy today. Love means to emotionally love sometimes, mostly when it is convenient and then to love only lovable people, if it is good for us. "Lord" means that someone is our Master usually when we tire of doing our own thing, or when it would give us security and protection.

God, and all that He is, is absolute. He is holy- absolutely holy. Jesus is Lord at all times, forever. The Word is always true, without exception, under all circumstances. There is never variance to the things of God. He means exactly what He says, and does exactly what He promises - always.

When you have called Jesus "Lord, Lord," what did you mean? When you said that you would serve Him alone, what did you mean? When you say that you love as Jesus does, what do you mean? How does your life line up with the absolutes of His desires and the perfection of His Word?

# FROM OUR FATHER'S HEART (A12)
## From Chapter 12 of "A White Stone"

The harvest is white right now,
but My church is so busy doing good things
that they can't see My things to do.
I ask you,
when did My gospel call you to any activity
that did not have the eternity of the souls of men and women
as its purpose?
When did I ever ask you to protect your rights?
Where in My Word does it say
that you must occupy your time doing works
that have no impact on the salvation of your enemies?
I am not in the midst of your projects of men.
The ultimate purpose of these doctrines of men
is the preservation of your freedoms,
your way.
I have set you free My way,
so that you might share My light
in the darkest places
for the good of those in bondage.
How pitiful and powerless your works are.
You have chosen this day whom you will serve.
All projects that have fleshly motives will fail.
I call them wood, hay and stubble
about to be burned away.
Some of you will stand empty-handed before Me on that day.
You think that your arms are full to present offerings to Me.
Your offerings are barren
and of no eternal worth.
Turn to Me.

*Remember My desires.*
*I care about the souls of those that are perishing.*
*You care about preserving your life*
*and call it My desire for you.*
*It is not Me you are listening to.*
*Turn now*
*to My purposes.*

Bible Correlations

*Luke 19:10;   Gal.3:3;   Eph. 2:8-9;*
*1 Pe. 2:9;   Rev. 3:15-17*

After we ourselves are saved, most of us forget the real reason that Jesus died on the cross. We remember that He died for us, but somehow that thought starts to consume us as we begin to work through "stuff" from then on. We take on a mentality that's all about us.  His priority, the souls of others, gets lost in this day-to-day personal survival mentality.

Our Bible, the living Word of God, calls us to follow in ⸎⸎⸎ ⸎⸎⸎⸎ Lord. Since it would be safe to assume that the

Lord means what He says, it might be a good idea to imagine what He would do in every given situation before we make our daily decisions.

What would Jesus do if He really were inhabiting each of our bodies? If He actually possessed each of us to the point that He was in absolute control over every action that we took, how many of the things that we are involved in would we continue? What would He do about the rapist or the murderer? What should we do about them? How would He treat the ones that chose to hate Him and His ideals? How should we treat them?

The word "love" comes to mind.

# FROM OUR FATHER'S HEART (A13)
## From Chapter 13 of "A White Stone"

Do not despair
or lose heart
when I am taking you through a hard time.
Do not despise
or turn away from Me,
but rather run to Me with open arms.
Run into My open arms
and know that I will hold you close to Me.
In such times as these,
please understand
My purpose for you and My plans for you
(Jer. 29:11.)
I know the plans I have for you, declares the Lord.
Plans to prosper you and not to harm you.
Plans to give you a hope and a future.
Just learn to trust in Me.
Depend on Me.
Rest in Me
and know that I am in control of every situation of your life.
There is nothing that happens in your life
that I don't know about first
( Matt. 10:29-31.)
Put your trust fully in Me
and not in the things of this world.
Draw close to Me.
Spend time with Me.
Get to really know Me.

## Bible Correlations

Jer. 29:11;   Matt. 5:23-24;
Matt. 10:29-31;   2 Cor. 4:16-18


A good friend once said something that changed my attitude about this walk we call Christianity. He said, "It's not about us, it's about Jesus." Before that moment, without really knowing it, I had taken the posture that God's job was to make my life better. The encouragements in His Word, given  to help the broken to be healed enough to walk unassisted, became "rights" for me to demand  my comforts from  God. I did all kinds of good things, but deep down inside - somewhere next to where pride lives - I was thinking that He "owed" me.

When that small statement was amplified  to my spirit, my perspective  was changed forever. The "it's not about me" part didn't  sit well at first. That meant that I had to face the fact that everything that I had ever done was for my own good, even coming to Him for salvation. After that, He showed me that I was doing all kinds of stuff  to make me  look  good  to Him and to others. Kind of scary places to go, ya know.  We need to know  that He can be trusted, of course,  but when are we going to turn the corner and  walk  for  the sake of His work, not for our own good?

## FROM OUR FATHER'S HEART (A14)
### From Chapter 14 of "A White Stone"

Holiness,
denial of self,
sacrifice
and
the crucified life.
Why do you not seek them?
They are the true path to happiness.
You fight to protect those things you hold tight
and call it My work.
You walk without power
because you have not made Me
your source of power.
You are ineffective by My standards,
but your search to fulfill your personal needs
blinds you from seeing how barren your life really is.
In doing your work and calling it Mine,
you have become angry,
fearful
and in need of changing your world.
How foolish.
How vain.
I am seeking those who cherish holiness unto Me.
I will use those who turn from the world and its ways.
Despise those things which stop you
from giving up your life completely
to Me.

*Bible Correlations*

Ps. 6:1-2;   Ps. 24:3-5;
Isa. 58:6-7;
Eze. 12:2;   Eze. 44:15-16;
Heb. 12:14


Smith Wigglesworth, an evangelist from the early 1900's, would come into a train compartment and after a few moments, people would have to leave because the presence of God in him convicted them of their sins. He didn't preach or say anything, the possession that he allowed God to have of him was oozing from his very being and affecting those around him.

We don't even begin to get it. We spend the largest portion of our lives providing for our feathered nests and finally, if we have any time left over, it goes to God. Then we wonder why we are powerless to affect for eternity the people that God brings across our path.

Think about it. How many people have you been in contact with since you were saved? How many have seen Jesus, even a little bit, because of that contact? I'm not talking about today's version of Jesus - the fist-clenched, flag-waving, people-condemning Jesus. I'm talking about the One Who came to show us His Father, the One Who came to die for them. What is that comparison in light of Him oozing through our every pore?

*Fun, huh?*

## FROM OUR FATHER'S HEART (A15)
### From Chapter 15 of "A White Stone"

### The Knock

Jesus
comes to all of us
in individual fashion.
The most important thing
is that we accept Him
when He does knock on the door of our life.
Many of us do not acknowledge Him right away.
Our Lord,
being the merciful God that He is,
will continue to give us a chance for salvation.
He
may come to us directly
or
through someone
who
is a witness
in his daily Christian walk.
Whatever the means,
He does call all of us ...
All we need do
is
answer!!

## Bible Correlations

Ps. 119:110-112;   Acts 20:21;
2 Cor. 6:2;   Rev. 3:20

If you've entered into a relationship with Jesus, you've probably already reflected on the many instances when the Holy Spirit wooed you to a point of decision regarding that life-changing relationship with Him. You may even have become awestruck at the number of opportunities the Lord extended to you. His mercy is incomprehensible!

I can recall my first "official" opportunity to accept Jesus as my Savior (I was clueless regarding Lordship.) I looked at the person who presented Him to me as though she came from Mars. I told her that I was just fine where I was at. I also vowed to never visit her again. Years later, I had the joy of calling her to confirm that her prayers had been answered.

When I finally entered into a relationship with Jesus, I responded to an altar call. Again, I was clueless, but something beyond myself urged me out of my seat and down to the altar. I truly did not understand what I was doing, but I know now that it was God's timing. He knew that I was seeking truth and needed Him to show it to me. God started a work in me - much to my confusion, at the time - and it wasn't until almost eight months later that I joined a fellowship and started to discover what had happened to me.

The point is: man is never the one to initiate a relationship with Jesus Christ; and he is also not the one capable of entering into that relationship on his own. *The Holy Spirit woos each of us to get us to the point where we're capable of saying "yes." Then, the decision is ours. No one will be able to say, "I was never called," or "I never understood the choice."*

*Do you ever stop to wonder why you said "yes," when someone else said "no?" I do, and at those times, I can only marvel and express my gratitude for the mercy of God.*

## FROM OUR FATHER'S HEART (A16)
### From Chapter 16 of "A White Stone"

Wealth, power, fame,
all fall pale next to My glory.
Begin to see My glory
as something tangible and real in your life,
not simply a word,
an entity beyond reach for you.
My glory is coming back to My people.
Surrender fully to what I am doing in your life
and you will be a part of what I am doing in the end times.
Your only hope is My presence.
The world and all of its wisdom is soon to pass away.
Do not be distracted by how powerful it seems.
It is all a lie.
All is moving toward an end I have determined.
Do not be fooled.
Only in Me is there peace.
Only in Me is there the power to overcome.
Submit to what I am doing and you will be safe.

## Bible Correlations

Ps. 119:37;   John 17:22;   Rom. 8:37;
Rom. 12:1-2;   Eph. 5:27;   Phil. 3:20-21


It is so much easier to respond to that which we can see, hear, etc., rather than to those things which are unseen, seemingly intangible. We need faith in God and in His Word to believe that the unseen is our reality as a believer. Our only security is a full surrender to God, so that He might make His reality our reality. We need to turn away from that to which we've become accustomed, in order that we may experience our God and all that He is and all that He desires for us.

## FROM OUR FATHER'S HEART (A17)
### From Chapter 17 of "A White Stone"

I know that  this is hard for you to comprehend at times,
but your sins no longer exist as far as I'm concerned,
if you've turned them over to Me through Jesus.
Any failure you've had,
any wrong you've done or do
is no longer on heaven's register,
if you repent to Me.
My desire
is for you to walk in the liberty
that has been bought at great cost for you.
Do not be weighed down by worldly cares.
You cannot see Me clearly through guilt and fear.
I am a loving God ... You are My child.
Why do you resist My love?
Even if I am taking you through a trial,
it is for your good.
I know best.
Please know that I am with you through it;
as a father protects the first steps of an infant,
I shield you.
Just trust Me.
The power of My love can make a way.

## Bible Correlations

*Josh. 24:15;   Ps. 103:12-13;   Isa. 43:1-2;*
*John 1:29;   Gal. 5:1*


I've had the privilege of seeing the moment that the light of the Gospel actually became a reality to an alcoholic. Dead eyes instantly showed hope. They changed and became brighter as the new man was created from within.

In the future of that man there proved to be tremendous trials, possibly even as difficult as he'd had prior to his acceptance, because his sin had left its mark on his immediate world. Through it all, however, the knowledge that he had been forgiven gave him the strength to make it. In his great need, he at first gripped that hope just to make it from moment to moment. Then as the Lord proved Himself in trial after trial, my friend began to trust his God.

He got it. He got the message. It eventually sank deep into his inner being that the work that was done over two thousand years ago was effective for him. He got it and ran with it, never looking back. He was new and forgiven, and his life had purpose. He was accepted by God when everyone else, including himself, had given up. Do you get it?

# FROM OUR FATHER'S HEART (A18)
## From Chapter 18 of "A White Stone"

There is precious little time-
but it is enough!
There will soon come upon churches
a mighty and sovereign move of the Holy Ghost.
At first,
you will not believe your boldness
nor the power available to you!
But you will remember My visit,
and you will know that the Word of God
is mighty and beyond your understanding.
You will finally comprehend the spiritual weaponry
that has always been yours.
In this final hour,
the winning of souls is all that will matter.
The power of God entrusted to the church is not for consumption -
it is for battle.
The fires of Hell will never be quenched,
and the people all around you steadily march in its direction.
You must turn them back.
Trust Me,
obey My Word,
use My Name often
and you will turn many to righteousness.
Carefully mark your time -
there is not much remaining.

*Do not be shaken by what will soon come upon the earth.*
*Remember how you felt in My presence,*
*and how I have already told you*
*that I would never leave you*
*nor forsake you.*

Bible Correlations

Prov. 28:1;   Isa. 6:1,2a,3,5;
Hag. 1:5;   Matt. 24:14;   Matt. 28:18-20;
Mark 16:15-18;   2 Cor. 10:4;
Phil. 1:27

Whether you know it or not, you've been in training. As Green Beret training prepares soldiers for any possible battle situation, you - as a Christian - are doing the same. Just as their purpose is to overcome the enemy, our training teaches us to submit to our Lord that He might win our hearts. As they physically get in shape, we are shown our weakness so that the power of Jesus might rule in our innermost being.

Because of our need to maintain some form of comfort level, most of us fail to see that the difficult circumstances that we encounter are really opportunities to do some spiritual weight lifting. Our failures bring forth the humility needed to be able to submit to the "dunamis" (power) of God. (Our word "dynamite" comes from that Greek word. It tells of an unstoppable power from our Father to work on our behalf.) That kind of power moves things around.

We have a problem. We believe God less than the world does sometimes. We don't trust His promises to us and we doubt that He will exhibit His power on our behalf. Then when He does, our pride lets us take the credit for any good that is accomplished.

The time is so short that we need to rethink our whole lives. We need to examine our doctrines to find out what is true and what is false. We need to align ourselves with His truth, so that we will be able to receive His power to win others when He chooses to impart it to us.

Wouldn't it be a shame if all time was concluded and you could show little to Him when asked for crowns to lay at His feet? I don't want that to happen to me or to those who are within my impact range.

## FROM OUR FATHER'S HEART (A19)
### From Chapter 19 of "A White Stone"

The brightness in your eyes will soon reflect
the perfected work on the cross by My Son in you.
Your spirit of joyous praise will soon quiet
the blasphemous words
that defy Me to be the God that I Am.
Your holy presence
will make anyone who will not acknowledge
Jesus as the only Lord
too uncomfortable to remain where they are
physically or spiritually.
Who will be able to remain where they are
when they see the Living Christ as a plumb line in you,
My people?
Choices must be made; it will be life or death.
There will be no middle road
once My work is fulfilled in you,
so they can see Me and choose.
Do you see
how important it is that you surrender fully to Me?
Do you see
how important it is to set aside doctrines of man;
those that have an appearance of godliness
but deny the power of the Living God?
The only way anyone can really see
the power
I have created by the cross
is to see the change
in you.

As you walk in holiness,
in purity,
while remaining in your weak vessel;
they will know that such power
cannot come from within,
but by the One Who lives within you.
Draw close now.
Many lives depend
on you becoming what I desire of you.

Bible Correlations

Deut. 30:19-20;   Josh. 24:15;   Matt. 16:26a;
Rom. 8:29;   1 Cor. 1:27-29;   2 Cor. 4:7;
2 Ti. 3:5

Most of us come to God because of our great need. Our days are frittered away confirming His promises to us. After a time, we grow to the point of seeing the need all around us and attempt to do something about it. Even then, our good works become honor badges that we hold before the Lord so that He might be pleased with us.

These two examples are very much akin to a newborn baby and a teenager. The babe must consume all and can give little in return. The teen has something to give, but most of the time only after he himself is satisfied.

There comes a time, however, when those attitudes are no longer acceptable. It is a time of maturity. The adult that acts like a baby or a teen, is soon found out. His value and usefulness is minimized by his immaturity. There is no value or strength to function as a mature adult, so he is cast aside when adults are needed.

In the life with God, there is an adult attitude that cares only about the things of God. It belongs to the mature Christian. The world, the flesh and all else is of no consequence to the kind of follower that God wants.

When you stand still until you are told to move and then move only for the good of your Lord, you are in line with the Word of God. When your only purpose for taking your next breath is to do the will of God, you will see His desires clearly. When your deepest and only desire is to be in an intimate association with Jesus, and the last thing that you want to do is to leave His presence; God will be able to empower you with His presence, because He will be able to trust you.

## FROM OUR FATHER'S HEART (A20)
### From Chapter 20 of "A White Stone"

When did I ever say
that ease and comfort would be your lot?
Look into My Word.
Those that I called My Own,
those I held dear to My heart
at times had no place to live.
Even My Own Son had no comforts of this world.
You seek to satisfy your own needs
and call it My will for you.
I prosper you and you use it to pad your rest areas.
Do you not see that I cannot use you
with a heart that has grown cold?
The weight of your possessions
and lusts
and fears of loss
have nullified your testimony.
You look no different than the world.
Change your hearts now.
Turn from seeking Me for your own gain.
The selfless life is the life to which I have called you.
You gave Me everything.
Why do you take it back?
I want to use you for My purposes,
but you are too busy serving your own needs.

*The people perish
all around you
and you don't even look up from your toil.
You praise Me with your lips,
but your hearts are far, far from Me.
Return now,
that I might use you.*

Bible Correlations

*Deut. 8:10-18;
Ps. 119:36; Hag. 1:4;
Matt. 6:1-2a*

If our lot as Christians is to have a comfortable existence, then the first century believers, some of whom sat under the teachings of Jesus, didn't hear what He had to say.

Those fools went to the arena when they could have believed themselves into palaces. In their ignorance of the provision that was their inheritance, they sold all that they had so others would not have to go without. After doing so, they didn't understand that God owed them great wealth because of the seeds that they had sown. They even forgave the sinners that fed them to the lions, when all the time they had the power of God behind them to change their society, so that all the evil people would no longer be in control. They had the mandate to take over, purify the land, overcome all the sin and set up a government where just and fair laws would rule.

Instead, those simpletons lost their lives in vain. They could have had so much after having been known as disciples of Jesus; but they chose to die, nameless and forgotten in some arena or desolate town. Who's going to ever remember them? How could their lives have been used by God with such wimpy attitudes?

Could it be that they did not understand God's plan as well as we do? There are some pretty successful people in the church that are saying so. They must be right. God has blessed and prospered them, hasn't He? Isn't that the sure sign of a Godly ministry?

Or maybe God has changed. Maybe He had one plan for them and because we are more important to Him, He wants us to have more. Maybe He wants us to be so rich that we don't really need Him for all of our provision. Maybe He saw the error of His ways and now desires that we function as the world does. Maybe we really do deserve more than they did. Do you think so? Huh? Huh?

## FROM OUR FATHER'S HEART (A21)
### From Chapter 21 of "A White Stone"

Holiness is freedom for you.
When Jesus was with you on earth,
He never set His mind on the things of the earth.
My purposes and My goals were always His goals.
As He kept His heart on things above,
He walked through all earthly circumstances untouched.
Even on the cross, He was untouched.
There was no earthly power that put Him there.
Schemes and dreams of mere men
were of no effect,
for He was not moved by them.
That same freedom is yours if you trust in Me.
You need not be touched by that which is around you.
Surrender fully to Me.
Seek My purposes rather than your own.
Learn of Me and My ways.
Submit to My Spirit that you might be free.
The work that I plan for you is for your best interest.
Submit to it.
You, too, can be untouchable
if
you keep your eyes
on Me.

## Bible Correlations

*Ps. 91:1-2,7,9-13;*
*Matt. 11:29; John 5:19;*
*John 7:30; Col.3:1-2; Jas. 4:7-9*

Jesus died a violent death at the hands of men who vigorously hated Him. It is said that on His way to the cross, He was unrecognizable as a man because of what they had done to Him. The flesh on His body was in shreds and some of His internal organs were exposed. He had been whipped with cords that had bits of glass, sharp pieces of bone and bent nails knotted into them. Each time they struck Him and pulled the whip back after it wrapped around His body, flesh was torn from Him. All of the violence that Satan could muster through his vessels exploded upon our Savior. It was the devil's chance to destroy the One Who had come to destroy him, so you know that he took particular delight in his task. With all this, He was untouched by the circumstances.

You and I know that being untouched does not mean that He did not hurt or care or feel. It in no way suggests that the weight of all that was happening was lifted from Him physically. He bore our sins!

Jesus, however, came to die. His delight was to do His Father's will. His passion was to accomplish the task at hand for all who would benefit from His actions. He did it for us. The joy set before Him was to see us reunited with our Father. Nothing could sway Him from that. In fact, the worst thing that could have happened, as far as He was concerned, would have been for the people to not torture and crucify Him - that they would love Him as we would desire to be loved. Then, they would really have touched or affected Him and His true mission!

# FROM OUR FATHER'S HEART (A22)
## From Chapter 22 of "A White Stone"

I have sent My Son, Jesus Christ,
to die;
and I have raised Him from the dead
that the world might again be brought into fellowship with Me.
I have sent My Holy Spirit
to indwell
each one that might believe and submit wholly to Him.
He is to exhibit to a world dying and out of answers,
the only answer -
the life of Jesus -
and it is to be done through those who believe.
By His life in you, the believer,
others are to see how Jesus loved,
lived
and died so that they might not perish.
Your life is to be so empowered by My Holy Spirit
that the blind might look at it
and recognize the life of Jesus
and be brought to Him for their salvation.
Instead of them seeing Who My Son really is,
they see weak,
pitiful ramblings of moral finger pointing and self-righteous,
self-serving, religious bigotry.

The Name of My glorious Son
has been brought to such low esteem in the eyes of your world
because of your cold,
fruitless religion,
that they laugh at and mock Him
instead of calling Him Lord.
When will you hear what I have been telling you?
When will you stop your foolish,
powerless activity
and lock yourself up with Me
so that you might really exhibit the life of My Son,
empowered by My Holy Spirit?
Repent,
turn,
stop now!
I am waiting for you.

Bible Correlations

Isa. 1:13;   Isa. 58:9b-12;   Mal. 1:10;
John 3:16;   John 15:26-27;
1 Cor. 3:16;   Col. 1:27-28

I used to think that as a Christian I would be walking around and the Lord would do all these really cool things for the benefit of the people around me, but it would all have very little to do with me. It finally became clear that people being able to see who Jesus is had very much to do with me.

The messenger does have an effect on the receiving of the message. God could circumvent this, but He's chosen to incorporate us into His plans. How ingenious! He helps us to become like Jesus through His Spirit, so that we ourselves become the message. How could it be any different? Doesn't it make sense that the messenger must resemble the message in order for people to see the truth in a way they can comprehend it?

Be encouraged! Spend time in God's presence and become the message. Let's give the world a true picture of Who Jesus is.

## FROM OUR FATHER'S HEART (A23)
### From Chapter 23 of "A White Stone"

It is the close of a season.
I am marshaling My forces.
I am preparing hearts to be part
of the great army of the body of Christ.
Do you see how bold the enemy has become?
Do you see how he has attempted to disfigure the children
that are called by My Name?
A turning point is at hand.
A new awakening is in this land
and it must start with you.
Take hold of what you are in Me.
Begin to realize that all My promises are for you.
Understand though, that they are not for self and flesh
or your worldly needs.
I do desire that you have life more abundantly - yes!
Use that life to rise above -
look to the provisions I have given you
to be used for a greater need.
As I gather My army, your part will become increasingly clear.
Drop all preconceived notions
as to what you felt were the uses for My provisions,
and submit to Me with an open mind.
I have prepared you for a specific purpose.
The time is now -
you can be the one.
Do not limit Me,
for I have chosen you.

## Bible Correlations

Josh. 1:6-9;   Ps. 138:8;   Eccl. 3:1;
Jer. 29:11;   Matt. 10:38-39;   Matt. 19:29;
Eph. 2:6-7;   2 Ti. 2:3-4

The words " marshaling forces, great army and enemy,"
present to us a picture that is far different than the one that God
intends. We love to imagine ourselves as great victors who have
annihilated the enemies of God, presenting the spoils of the
glorious battle at His feet. It thrills us to think that one day, we
will be riding a magnificent white steed into the eternal sunset
with our Lord - battle-torn, weary, but proud.

The fact is, if the war that we imagine were a physical
war, Jesus wouldn't be with us as we rode proudly into the sunset.
He probably would be back on the smoky battlefield, bandaging the
wounds of our victims and cleaning up the carnage that was left
from our encounter. He would have cared for the souls of those
that we attempted to destroy by telling them once more of His
Father's love.

Come to think of it, isn't that what He is doing at this
very moment? Isn't He still working to have those that we have
blown off see what He has done for them? Isn't He healing all
of the wounds that we have caused by our interpretation of how to
fight for Him? When are we going to really understand His
ways? Is it not true that our Leader died so that others may
live?

## FROM OUR FATHER'S HEART (A24)
### From Chapter 24 of "A White Stone"

When I pour out My Spirit, it shall be as never before.
This world will know those that follow Me
for they shall be set apart;
no longer a laughing stock,
but a wonder.
But deceit will still abound,
and those stiff-necked ones will find a way
to justify their sins
and be hardened to even the largest move on My part.
Understand that it must be so.
Free will is a most misused gift, but it must be so.
Delight in Me for I am about to move in your life.
Much has been promised
in the short time you have known Me,
and all will come to pass.
I am pleased,
but seek My face as never before.
Do not worry about what is or is not happening,
for I am proud to orchestrate your life.
Learn to submit to My voice,
for you will need to know for sure
when I am talking and move instinctively.
For My Spirit is as a breeze
and then gone,
so know when it is My Spirit.

## Bible Correlations

Ps. 37:23; Prov. 3:5-6; Prov.16:9; Prov. 20:24;
Jer. 7:22-27; Jer. 9:4-6; Joel 2:28-29;
John 3:8; John 10:14-16;
2 Ti 3:13

Can you imagine an army of believers laying down their lives for the ones who hate them and are attempting to control them in some way? Could you see the impact of a kind, loving word that is empowered with the presence of God, breaking through the fury of an aggressor? What a glorious picture to imagine the whole church of God moving in unison, listening only to their Master, caring only for His cares, loving as He loves and living in His power.

Try to picture the havoc evoked when chains can't contain, words can't intimidate, pain can't dissuade and death is met joyfully. Seek to envision millions of people functioning in a peace that defies the circumstances, a power that is unstoppable, a love that is undeniable and a mission that can't be understood. How does one fight against that kind of warfare, when the other side only knows tools of aggression used in their kind of war?

I know that the picture that was just painted is generally considered to be an endtime portrait because it is so far from what the church is today. What is not easily understood, is why each of us is not living that kind of life today. We have all been told to do so. Why haven't we obeyed our Master? Pretty funny, huh?

## FROM OUR FATHER'S HEART (A25)
### From Chapter 25 of "A White Stone"

Do not fear the giants in the land.
The largest and biggest giant in your eyes
is simple and small in Mine.
The most powerful people with the loudest voices
are only a ruptured vessel or stopped heart away
from being silenced.
All is at My control,
even though it looks like I have lost control.
I don't move through worldly, visible power.
I don't move through logic and reason.
I move as I see fit for My purposes to be accomplished.
My weapons are not and have never been
those the world understands.
Fire,
wind,
cold
and earth movements
cause change and are warnings.
Weakness,
humility,
forgiveness
and love
are My way of doing much good.
Be sure to see through the plans of man,
and remember the plans
that I have ordained from the beginning.

As they unfold in My perfect timing,
do not be surprised by the blindness
of this
generation -
even My people.
Those that have not heard, will not hear.
Those that would not see,
will not be able to see.
Surrender fully to My will and My Word.
It is the only safe place
to find sure steps in the coming times.

Bible Correlations

1 Sam. 17:45-49;   2 Sam. 5:24;   2 Chron. 20:15-23;
Ps. 32:7-8;   Joel 3:10;   Matt. 13:12-16;
1 Cor. 1:27;   1 Cor. 10:4;
Phil. 2:4-5;   1 John 2:6

So often, our thinking runs horizontally when it really needs to move vertically. If we keep our eyes on people and circumstances, there is a great temptation to try to find our own solutions, which brings inadequate results, at best.

Have you ever noticed how often God's solution to something doesn't match the way you figured things would or should turn out? Why should we be surprised? His Word says that His thoughts and ways are not ours. (If they were, we'd no doubt also take credit for whatever He did as well as for what we do.) However, God never intended that there be a distinction between His thoughts and ways and ours. Man caused the distinction in the Garden of Eden. When the Lord says that His thoughts are not ours, it was another way of saying that man turned his back on Him.

So, the next time things appear to be going wrong, try to remember one thing - nothing slips past God. That one thought can make an incredible difference in any given situation because your next thought is, "OK, what is He doing?," and then your focus is where it needs to be and you'll find your solution. It usually turns out to be God Himself.

## FROM OUR FATHER'S HEART (A26)
### From Chapter 26 of "A White Stone"

There will come a time
when My anointed will walk in freedom,
having no bonds or entanglements
with the world.
It will be a time
when those devoted to Me and Me alone
will rise above all of the restrictions and sin
that have held My bride captive.
Those that have chosen to scoff
at the things which I hold dear
will no longer be able to do so.
They will see with their own eyes,
a people that make My world come alive -
living testimonies of the true gospel.
Choices will need to be made by all people;
either they will submit to the truth of My Word
and become part of My true church,
or they will deny Me in those
that are before their very eyes.
When My anointing falls on My bride -
those that have sold out to Me during this time of testing -
there will be no doubt as to who belongs to Me.
Purity, holiness,
devotion, mercy, power:
all of My fruits and gifts
in fullness
will be manifest in and through
the humble,
the meek, the lowly in spirit.

My Word will pierce the hungry soul
as My people
live and move
and have their being in Me.
I have told you of a salvation
to be revealed
in the last time.
I have told you of a great harvest.
Now I am about to equip those Whom I can trust.
Be part of My bride.
Give everything to Me.
Devote yourself to My ways and My desires.
Respond to this call, My beloved.
Do not turn away and be left outside.
I love you
and would love for you to be equipped
to help bring forth the harvest.
Choose to be completely Mine now.
The time is short.

Bible Correlations

1 Ki. 18:21;   Ps. 10:4;   Matt. 5:3-16;
Matt. 9:37-38;   Matt. 10:32-33;   Heb. 12:1-2;
2 Pe. 3:5;   Rev. 12:4;   Rev. 13:16-17

Jesus, the Master and Lord of all, will not take a whore as His bride. Disloyal, wavering individuals with divided interests will not be part of the wedding feast. Could you imagine a time in the eternal future, long after the present has unfolded, when a member of Jesus' bride would decide not to be in full accord with the orchestration of some event He has decided to accomplish? Any rebellion at that time would be unthinkable. The elimination of any hint of disorder during that time is the purpose for the time in which we now live. God has planned that His priests and kings will rule in full accord with His every wish to accomplish future creations. There is no room in the plan for rebellion.

We are so short-sighted. We cannot think past our limited perspective. If this life and future streets of gold (where we exist in some wandering state of euphoria) were all that our Lord had for us, the salvation, purification, devotion and commitment process that we are experiencing, at present, would have little purpose. God is now searching for those who will commit fully to Him. Future creations will know of our generations as we know of the angels. There will be no rebellion this time, however. That is being worked out right now with you and me. When we are sealed, and have proven our desire to be faithful and show a determination to walk in His holiness, we will be with God forever as we join Him in purposes and plans that are far bigger than we could ever imagine.

## FROM OUR FATHER'S HEART (A27)
### From Chapter 27 of "A White Stone"

My wrath is soon to break forth upon your land.
There will be no place to hide
for those who have not heard My call to holiness.
But fear not!
Those who know Me,
who have learned to be locked up with Me,
will rise above the darkest places.
I will have My bride.
The world will see and notice
the redemptive power of the cross.
They will be astonished
as I bring forth the beauty of life from the ashes.
My Word will go forth.
My plans will be accomplished.
My people will be vessels of honor to Me.
Be of great courage.
Be steadfast.
Lock yourselves up with Me and live.

Bible Correlations

Isa. 14:24;   Isa. 30:18 liv;   Isa. 60:1-2;
Isa. 61:3;   Zech. 7:13;
John 15:13;   Rev. 6:14-17

Let's say that all we read in the Bible is as simple and as profound as mankind being given a chance to decide whether he wants to be with God forever or not; that all of the stories, covenants and situations are steering each of us to the point of deciding to freely serve Him. If this premise is plausable, then it stands to reason that all situations that mankind faces are simply orchestrated to bring him to that end. To carry the thought further, God is positioning everything to fit a determined end.

Obviously, the biblical scenario is far more complex than even the most learned of His people can understand, but what is very clear is the fact that God is very active in the affairs of man. He devises means, creates situations and causes circumstances so that His plans will be completed.

Typically, He woos His people to Himself, allows hardships to occur if they don't come and brings devastation if they remain hardhearted - all for the purposes of bringing each of us to a state of surrender. Those who respond freely are safe. Those who remain hardened to His love are given every chance possible, no matter what has to be done to bring them to helpless submission. Those who resist all, will have chosen to be separated from Him forever. They are allowed to remain with their free choice of fathers.

## FROM OUR FATHER'S HEART (A28)
### From Chapter 28 of "A White Stone"

The lusts of the flesh and the pride of life
allow the enemy to gain access to you.
They make you vulnerable to attack
by opening the door to any form of fear and oppression.
You <u>must</u> overcome them.
There is hidden sin in your heart.
Remove it by repenting of it to Me.
Let the light of My Holy Spirit shine on it.
Confess it as sin and turn from all entertainment of thoughts,
sights or habits.
Renew your mind daily with My Word,
My thoughts
and My presence;
and you will be set free.
You turn away from sin
and I will be there for you;
but you must turn away.
Each time a thought is noticeable, cast it down.
Stop looking in the direction of sin.
Stop holding it dear for it has no place in you.
You are Mine and I want you spotless.
I am jealous for that area of your heart.
Come to Me and be holy.
In My holy fire,
any presence of evil will be consumed.
I am your safety,
your strong tower, your haven.
I am your consuming fire.

I require you this day –
to return to your first love,
your consuming love for Me,
the desire for My Word
and the power that is Mine.
You know Me.
Now begin to believe again.
Flee from fear.
It no longer has a hold on you.
I have cut its cord, so turn from it.
You are Mine and nothing will take you from Me.
Be intense for My presence
and
My presence alone.

Bible Correlations

Ex. 33:15;   Ps. 61:3;
Ps. 63:1;   Rom. 12:12;   1 Cor. 4:5;
2 Cor. 4:4;   Heb. 12:29

In Exodus 33:15, Moses asks the Lord not to send him anywhere if the presence of the Lord does not go with him. He continues to proclaim the truth that the presence of the Lord is the only way that people will distinguish the difference between those who have found favor with God and those who haven't. What profound truth on one hand and what an incredible indictment to this generation on the other. We not only don't fear entering any arena without the presence of our Lord, few of us even know how to begin to recognize the true presence of God, let alone achieve it. Most of us are so far removed from experiencing God, that we run to every function that claims to have an anointing, or a man of God present or power of any sort. It is shameful to see what the people who call themselves God's children will acknowledge to be His presence and anointing.

Saul of Tarsus understood the presence of God. He was unable to stand, went blind and lived his entire life, desiring to spend it continually in God's presence. His initial experience with God was by no means fun, but it was real enough to let him desire to die to anything that would hinder God from taking complete control of him. An instant involved with the truth of God destroyed even the most treasured lie of the enemy.

My prayer is that we crave the presence of God, knowing that it will consume every fiber of our being. I pray that we really desire to cease to exist as we are.

## FROM OUR FATHER'S HEART (A29)
### From Chapter 29 of "A White Stone"

My children
who thrive on and desire only intimacy with Me
are about to be empowered with My presence.
Those who have turned away
from their useless flurry of activity to change the world
are about to enter into a spiritual understanding
that will allow them to again represent My Son,
Jesus,
to their world.
People will recognize My Son through their lives.
They will see Him
and have to choose between life or death
because of the convicting power
of a wholly surrendered vessel of honor
that contains My Holy Spirit.
Who can deny what has been done for all mankind
when it becomes visible through the lowly,
the weak,
the surrendered,
the children?
I will not use the dead, the empty and the proud.
I never have and will not start now.
Whitewashed containers
full of dead men's bones
have no place in the economy of spiritual power.
I have called you.
Now I am about to empower those who have come.

## Bible Correlations

Matt. 5:16;   Matt. 23:27-28;
1 Cor. 15:54b-55;   1 Pe. 5:5-6;   Rev. 3:1-2

God will use those who desire intimacy with Him. How could it be any other way? How else could we possibly become like Jesus except in the presence of our God? If we don't pursue an intimate relationship with our God, we won't be able to represent Jesus to the world. They won't see Him because of our flesh, our pride. God doesn't operate in that realm.

Smith Wigglesworth would be in a group of people and his mere presence would cause some of them to want to flee from him. They were convicted of their sin because of the presence of God housed in a surrendered vessel.

If we cling to the world, we cannot represent Jesus. We can only represent what the world already knows. We can only represent death, not life, because we have crowded out real life - our Lord Jesus. He is the way, the truth and any real life. Our mixed messages come from attempting to serve two masters - both the world and God. Messengers with that kind of mix will always bring death to the already dying.

It really is time to stop trying to ride the fence. If you want to be used by God, sell out to Him now. Do what it takes to be like Jesus in every way, to everyone, always.

## FROM OUR FATHER'S HEART (A30)
### From Chapter 30 of "A White Stone"

Holy ground is important to Me.
There is no way for the unclean to enter in and harm you
if I have girded My guardians around My places.
However, My back must be turned,
and My guardians must create breaches
when vice is invited into My holy places by My children.
Violations of My Word,
or the spirit of My Word,
by relaxed attitudes and thoughtless conversation
bring forth harm and breach the safety of My protection.
Guard your words.
Guard your relationships.
Guard your hearts
so that I might maintain My presence in your midst.
Because you are My children,
there is no place that you are not safe
if I have called you there,
because I am there with you.
No one can intrude upon a place that I have established for you,
if My presence is hallowed and welcome.
However,
be assured that I am calling you to be watchmen
over your words
and your actions.
That way I will be able to join you in all that you do,
wherever you are,
for your good
and My glory.

## Bible Correlations

*1 Ki. 8:61;*
*Isa. 35:8-9;   Matt. 12:34-35;*
*Matt. 16:18b;   Rev. 2: 9a &10a*


I was once told that in the spiritual realm, we are surrounded by hosts of God dedicated to protecting us from any harm. At no time can the enemy pass that globe of protection. The spirits of lust, fear, anger or any other harmful agent are helpless to intrude into this powerfully protected area. They must remain outside and harmless to us. Harmless, that is, unless we choose not to move according to the commands of the Word of God. Any time that we willingly choose to entertain any spirit that is not of God, these protective forces must obey our wishes, and allow for a breach in the perimeter so that whatever we choose to invite in can have access to us. The more that we allow this to happen, the easier that spirit is able to enter.

I am not sure how accurate this picture really is. I am sure though, that it portrays a concept that is well worth remembering. It is well known that our Lord is more than ready to come to our rescue in times of trouble and also that He will never leave us or forsake us. We, however, have a free will to do as we please, to entertain whatever our hearts desire. Our choice will be the difference between eventual life or death.

## FROM OUR FATHER'S HEART (A31)
### From Chapter 31 of "A White Stone"

I have called you to a Holy Place
that cannot be touched by those that would come against you.
You, however,
take deep concern at the seeming power demonstrated
by those that oppose My Word.
If you would only receive what I have for you.
If you would only look to Me,
get to know Me,
listen to what I have said and am saying,
you would never fear again.
How could you be afraid after you have seen Me?
How could you be afraid after you have beheld My power?
I have called you to an intimate relationship with Me
so that you may come to know Me,
but you do not come.
I wait and you do not come.
I prepare a feast and you eat from the streets.
If only you could see.
If only you could learn that I have not called you
to a place of fear and need.
I have called you to a Holy Place –
a place filled with Me,
where all of your needs are met.
It is a place that cannot be affected by the world around you.
Come.
Come and learn of Me.
Come to My Holy Place.

## Bible Correlations

Ps. 23:5a;   Ps. 27:1-6;   Ps. 81:13-16;
Isa. 30:18 liv;   Rev. 19:9a

Our enemy is a dirty fighter. He plays by his own rules and employs any trick to prove himself stronger than God to us. From the so-called cartoons that we are exposed to at a very early age, to movies, to his agents that we meet and every day's experience in between, he parades his prowess before us. We are aliens in his world and cannot avoid some form of contact with his ways at almost any given moment of the day. It is said that if something is repeated often enough, with enough energy, it will become truth to those that are exposed to it, no matter how untruthful it is.

What is quite confusing is that the church knows the tactics and ultimate desires of the enemy of God, and still chooses to remain in his realm, vulnerable to his lies for the majority of each day. We spend the mandatory fifteen to twenty minutes with our God each morning, and expect that to make us impervious to the lies for the rest of the day. We are not only void of any armor, but we are lacking the awareness that we are naked. Is it any wonder that we are weak and powerless to overcome the temptations that hound us at every corner? Our lives as warriors would be pretty comical, if they weren't so shameful.

## Section B

The following pages contain messages from the heart of our Father that were published within the context of conversation in the companion novel "A White Stone."

Originally, they were words given in prayer long before "A White Stone" was written, as were all of the others in this book. During the writing of "A White Stone," however, I felt led to use them as conversation by the characters in the novel. I am thrilled to see how the Holy Spirit empowered them with His life, all the while maintaining the unity and integrity of the storyline.

You might note that the words were given and kept for some time before they were used, a few of them almost ten years. The question arises then as to the intention of the Holy Spirit for them. Were they given in prayer to act upon in real life, or were they given specifically for use within the context of the book?

If my personal opinion matters, I believe that they line up with what the Holy Spirit is saying loudly to the children of God this very moment. I believe that the spirit, content and exhortations are very much in line for each of us to take to heart.

Oh, the wonder of our God! To provide material at a given time, knowing that it would have the most impact even as much as ten years later.

## FROM OUR FATHER'S HEART (B1)
### Taken from a conversation on page 130 of
### " A White Stone"

A time is coming,
and is now here
when My people will feel the wrath of their sin
and neglect of Me.
For too long,
they have been blemished by the world and its ways.
Watch as My Word goes forth
to purge and to purify.
What looks to the unskilled in My Word
as persecution by the enemy
is really My hand upon them to cleanse their lives.
Too many have called themselves Mine,
but choose to stay in the world.
Walk above anything that resembles
the ways that seem right to man
for its end is death.
Holiness unto the Lord
is the only heart that will prevail.
Faith coming from fellowship with Me
will be the only answer
to all the needs
of those who walk with Me.
I will be Lord,
and now the world will see Me
through those who are purified
by the coming fire.

*Bible Correlations*

2 Sam. 14:14;
Prov. 14:12;   Jer. 1:12 amp;
Matt. 6:24;   2 Ti. 3:12;   Heb. 12:14;
( Interesting spin - Mark 4:16,17 amp)


We can't have it both ways. If we choose the world's ways, we will   experience the consequences of our sin. We will be distancing ourselves from God whether we realize it or not.

Thank You, Father, that You are not content to leave us in our simultaneous pursuit of opposites. Thank You for devising means to draw us solely to You.  Thank You for Your Word, that it is literally at work in us to change us and make us more like Jesus. Thank You for all forms of persecution; that they are not just something that happens to us, but that they accomplish something in us. Thank You for holiness, that the world might see Jesus through us.

## FROM OUR FATHER'S HEART (B2)
### Taken from a conversation on page 154 of
### "A White Stone"

My people have for too long
called for My anointing to fall upon them
without submitting their lives to a walk of purity.
It will no longer be.
Only the pure in heart will be entrusted with My power.
Only the holy unto Me will be given My rhema Word.
Only those dead to the world
will see the manifestation of grace in their lives.
I have called and few have heard.
I have warned and few have heeded.
I have exhorted,
and still My people go about their own business,
and sometimes even call it Mine.
Soon that will end.
No more.
My gifts are without repentance, yes;
but My presence must accompany those gifts,
or they will fall to the ground.
You will now see who is pure in heart.
Watch. Watch and be amazed
at what I am about to do in My Church.
It will no longer resemble the church of the world
when I am finished purifying it.
It will be holy.
It will be pure.
It will serve no other gods.
Now it is full of whoredoms,
but soon it will be My bride.

## Bible Correlations

### Eze. 44;    Matt. 22:14;    1 John 2:6 & 20

What is an anointing? It's being set apart and empowered by the Holy Spirit (symbolized by the anointing oil) for a particular work in serving God. (It's interesting to note that anointing was also a way to prepare the dead for burial. Shouldn't we be "dead," so to speak, so that the anointing of God can flow freely in us without our flesh getting in the way?)

The anointing, however, is not cheap. We have to pay the price, and it will cost us everything. Are we willing to do God's will in all things? When Jesus says, "few are chosen," is this not more a matter of our choice, rather than God's, that this is true? We must walk the talk; nothing less is sufficient any longer. If we represent Jesus, we must look like Him!

If you look in Ezekiel 44, you'll notice two priesthoods mentioned. The Abiathar priesthood could only minister to the people because they strayed from the one true God and turned to idols. What takes God's place in our lives? Praise God for His mercy which allows us to repent and choose to be single-minded and of one heart. How else can we be the bride?

As we daily reaffirm our choice to serve God and Him only, we will be like the Zadok priesthood, who were allowed to minister to God and experience His presence because they stayed true to Him. Why would we want to do anything apart from the anointing of God?

## FROM OUR FATHER'S HEART (B3)
### Taken from a conversation on page 153 of
### "A White Stone"

I extend My grace
to all of My children,
but I ask you to choose this day
whom you will serve.
Each of you has been hearing My call to you
for many months, even years.
Some of you
have applied My words to your lives
in differing degrees.
Those of you
who have understood the signs all around you
and discerned the times
in which you live
have made the decision to lay your lives down before Me
that I might accomplish My total work in you.
Some of you,
however,
have not chosen to recognize the times and seasons,
and have remained in service to yourselves,
doing self-motivated good works
in My Name.
You must take this time to repent
or you will not be part of the soon outpouring
of My Holy Spirit
for His end time work.

## Bible Correlations

### Josh. 24:15;  John 12:24-26;  Rom. 12:1

In the matter of spiritual things, the choice is always ours. I find that to be a sobering and scary thought, but it always drives me back to the Lord in the knowledge of how desperately I need Him. What a great, safe place to be!

Know that God is moving on regardless of whether or not we move with Him! His desire is to include us. What is ours? It's time to be honest with God and with ourselves.

Here's your choice:  Love your life now and lose it eventually, or hate your life in this world (don't focus on it continually, don't be concerned for it) and preserve it forever  by seeking the Father and His will.  You will also see others come to that same position because you laid  your life down.  Easier said than done, isn't it?  It always is, but that's where God's marvelous grace and mercy come to the rescue.  As the song goes,  "... no one else can touch my heart like You do."

## FROM OUR FATHER'S HEART (B4)
### Taken from a conversation on page 150 of
### "A White Stone"

There is time,
but not so much as you might think;
time to be conformed to My Word.
My Word was given to you simply and clearly.
You have made it confusing and difficult
by constantly attempting to make it suitable for your purposes.
Does not My Word declare that it is sent
to accomplish My purposes?
All of you are really Mine.
I have bought you at a great price,
but you live daily as if you belong to no one.
You rob Me of many hours that could be used
to tell others of My love,
just to retain your comfort.
Everything that you claim for your own is really Mine.
I don't need it for I own all things,
but I want you to invest your first fruits in Me.
The tithe is not a tax to you,
but a sowing into what will be.
You have robbed Me and think that I haven't noticed.
I know what is about to come upon this earth
and some of you have not invested
in the power that you will need to overcome.
Soon you will see that My Word
and My principles work better
than your own devices.
To the faithful, remain faithful;
only you will stand.

*Only you will see My rewards in life to come.*
*Remember what a few loaves and fishes turned into*
*when willingly placed into My hands?*
*That is but a shadow of what is sent ahead and stored for you.*
*Search My Word.*
*One day it will search you.*
*On that day, you will be before Me.*
*Only what My Word says will matter then.*
*My Word is your only standard for holiness,*
*faithfulness, obedience, love and all other issues.*
*My Word reveals to you what I love,*
*what I hate*
*and*
*what I require.*
*There is still time.*
*I encourage you to humble yourselves before Me*
*and allow My Spirit to make your hearts tender.*
*Settle the issue of obedience forever.*
*Seek Me right now. My blood still covers.*
*My grace still avails.*
*My love never ceases to call out to you.*

Bible Correlations

1 Chron. 16:23;   2 Chron. 6:2;
Isa. 55:8-12;
Mal. 3:8-12;   John 6:1-13;   John 12:47-48;
Rom. 12:1-2;   Rev. 3:14-22;
Rev. 22:18-19

I wonder how we would react if someone that vowed to devote his life and all that he had to us, would function in the same manner that we relate to our Lord?

On the other hand, what if we made an alliance with someone that contractually made it look like we had to hold to our agreement and fulfill its stipulations, even if the other party did not? How would we feel if they purposely violated every aspect of it? To top it all off, let's say that they came to us daily to demand that we fulfill our part, even while they were in the midst of reneging on their promises. Making matters worse, they insisted to us and every one else that they were more than fulfilling their part of the agreement. How would we feel? What would we do if we loved them?

Let's say, however, that in the beginning, their private counsel in charge of examining the contract (a Laodicean lawyer) had unknowingly misinterpreted the terms of the agreement to them. In his zeal to please and in his own ignorance, he covered only the positive benefits and never touched on the repercussions should they violate any of the terms included. How would we feel toward them then? What would we do if we really loved them?

Our Father in heaven is calling us to re-examine our actions, commitments and contract. Out of love, patience and mercy, He is warning us of the repercussions of our actions when we violate His contract, even if we are acting that way because we have listened to someone else's interpretation of its content. Maybe it is time for us to start to listen, learn from the Word and then honor what we said we would do.

## FROM OUR FATHER'S HEART (B5)
*Taken from a conversation on page 151 of*
*"A White Stone"*

Many of you
have been entrusted with much
to be used for My work
during the short life I have given you.
You have, however,
consumed most of what you have been given –
whether that be money,
talent, influence, education or any other gifting–
upon your own lusts.
Your gifts are not really gifts,
as you suppose,
but simply the returning to Me
what was never really yours.
All was rightfully Mine in the first place.
You have been put in charge
of what I have given you,
as hired shepherds of sheep would have been,
but you have sold My property for your own gain.
You have been found out,
and now are being called to account.
This day you must make a choice:
serve the Lord Jesus Christ alone
and be part of the great harvest,
or serve the world
and its materialism.

## Bible Correlations

### Eze. 34:2-10;   Matt. 6:24;   Luke 12:48b;
### Acts 5:1-11

I wonder what Ananias and Sapphira would have done with the rest of their lives if they lived under the grace that we somehow have been given? Would they have been elected to some prominent position in the early church because of their perceived generosity by undiscerning people? Maybe they would have had some business cards printed (on parchment of course,) and become widely accepted, traveling evangelists, proclaiming the glories of God.

An interesting note to all of this light-hearted, possibly inappropriate, conjecture is the fact that the amount of grace that He chose to give them would not have changed His heart as God, no matter how it may have been perceived. He would have been just as displeased with the impurity of their sacrifice, just as unhappy with their attitude toward His Holy Spirit; just as justified to strike them dead. The church at the time, and Ananias and Sapphira themselves, would have been clueless as to His real attitude toward them, simply because of their apparent prosperity. No one would have been aware of how they had displeased God.

So then, do you believe that your life is pleasing to God simply because you have been prospered and deemed important in your small circle, or is it time for you to drop to your knees in repentance and awesome fear of your God? Maybe a little thankful praise for His mercy would be a good idea right before you change your ways, too, huh?

## FROM OUR FATHER'S HEART (B6)
*From an interaction on page 109*
*of "A White Stone"*

*These days*
*are the beginning of the end of time as you know it.*
*If you choose to listen and open your eyes*
*to the season that you live in,*
*you will soon see My hand in action*
*to change My church.*
*All who come close to hear from Me now*
*will see Me*
*and know Me*
*as I had originally intended for My people*
*from the beginning.*
*It is about to happen all over the world as My plans go forth.*
*Be ready.*
*Be prepared.*
*It will happen soon and speedily.*
*I have already begun,*
*and no man will change*
*what I have set in motion.*

*Bible Correlations*

*Isa. 43:13;   Hab. 1:5;   Hab. 2:3;*
*Zeph. 1:7;   Hag. 2:6-7;   Heb. 12:26-29*

One day, possibly early in the morning, a worn sandal touched the edge of the Jordan river. The time had come for the next portion of the plans of God to be set in motion. Quietly, with no fanfare except for the comments made by John, the baptizer, the eternal consequences of people's choices from that time onward would be made known to them. The people who lived in that time period would need to conform to the plan that unfolded before them, whether they wanted to or not. Their lives had changed from that very moment. No one could stop what had been set in motion. This season in the plan of God will continue until He says it's over.

Shortly before this season concludes, it is generally believed that an application of grace will be available to the end generation of people, so that they might reveal to the world the true character of Jesus Christ. It is also an accepted teaching that there will be a wooing, or heralding, to draw intimately close to Jesus for those Christians who choose to be a part of that move of God, shortly before the final call.

For several years now, the discerning ones within the church have sensed that particular wooing to holiness; an exhortation to deep repentance; a bridal call to single-heartedness and complete submission to the will of God. Make no mistake, as sure as the times changed when that sandal of the Messiah was on the edge of the Jordan, the present times will change when the Lord decides to finalize His current bridal call. Have you responded? Maybe you should consider doing so before He says "enough, all is completed."

## Section C

This section contains  words from the heart of the Father that were used in  "A White Stone Workbook." The workbook was published in response to  requests by people who had finished the novel "A White Stone."

After hearing the call to holiness proclaimed in that novel, the general question was, "Where do I go now?" The study of the traditional bride waiting for her groom,  character study of Jesus and the pursuit of the commitment to become like Him was the logical response.

Once again, the Lord proves Himself to be constant in His call to holiness, as these words were written over a span of  fifteen years. Test them to see if they are not pertinent for use in  the pursuit of holiness even today.

Please note: The words do not follow the same sequence as in  the workbook.

## FROM OUR FATHER'S HEART (C1)
### From page A31 in "A White Stone Workbook"

Are you going to do what I tell you to do?
Are you going to live before people
as the finest example of mankind did -
in total obedience to His God and Lord?
If not, what is your relationship with Me all about?
Why do you come to tell Me how much you love Me -
that you serve Me -
and then function according to the dictates
of your fleshly desires?
Why do you tell Me that you have made Me your priority,
and then allow your own will
to be the god that you serve?
The world lies,
but they have never said that they could be trusted.
Their father is the father of lies.
They break their commitments,
but they always have,
and always will be like that.
But you ...
you are Mine ...
you represent Me.
You have taken My Name as your God.
You have proclaimed aloud
that you are Mine through My Son, Jesus,
and still you go about breaking all of the commitments
that you make,
even to Me.
It is now time to repent.
Turn from your ways and become a student
of the ways of My Son.
Be known to others as He would be known.

*Walk in His integrity,*
*no matter what the cost may be to you.*
*Your continual choosing of His ways*
*over your ways will bring the fragrant oil*
*of the Holy Spirit to those who need to savor it.*
*That oil will be with you*
*because it will be needed*
*to heal the wounds you encounter through your obedience.*
*If you say that you follow My Son,*
*you will acquire the scars that He did.*
*Those scars will be the testimony of your commitment to Me.*
*The desires and compassions of Jesus*
*will be given only to those*
*who have walked and conducted themselves as He did.*
*Through the denial of who you are,*
*I will make you Who He is to others.*
*Those who are lost will again see Who Jesus is*
*because you will be in their midst*
*as My waiting bride.*
*Turn away from your ways to My ways now.*
*Deny yourself of all that is not like Jesus.*
*Come to Me*
*to be changed*
*and we will walk together.*

Bible Correlations

Matt. 15:6b-11; Matt. 23:27-28;
John 15:18-21, 27; 2 Cor. 2:14; 1 John 2:6

Have you ever been in the presence of someone who has overcome extreme hardship - someone who went through life and death situations, intense physical or emotional trauma and did more than survive the ordeal; they prospered, having gained much more than if nothing had happened? Do you remember how when meeting them, you knew that there was some powerful, almost unconquerable strength about them that made you somewhat envious? I don't mean envious of them per se, but envious of the inner qualities that they possessed? You may not have desired to go through what they had been through, but it would have been nice to possess the strength that they gained from the experience. If that same person was also gifted with uncompromising integrity, there might even have been a sense of awe in meeting them.

In a small way, that very kind of inspiration, amplified thousands of times, is what the bride of Christ is supposed to be presenting to the world. The persona of Jesus, the fragrance of heavenly ointment should be wafting from each of us, and landing wherever it is needed, carrying with it the desire to gain it at any cost.

That kind of gift to the world will cost you everything. It will come only from great pressure and humbling hardship. The death of our old self will be required to gain it. Jesus will have to be more than your Savior. He must be your everything.

# FROM OUR FATHER'S HEART (C2)
## From page B75 in "A White Stone Workbook"

For a long time now,
I have called you to be like My Son, Jesus -
to be complete in Me -
but you have refused to listen.
You have chosen to remain in your sinful nature,
denying My power to change you.
You have a form of godliness,
but you do not let Me complete the work
that is necessary to show the world My Son,
Jesus.
Soon the Holy Spirit will be moving
in a direction that is new
to those who haven't chosen My ways.
He will execute My bold judgments
to make you bend to My ways,
instead of allowing you to continue in your ways.
There will no more be
the kind of grace from Me
that has allowed you to be less
than I have determined for your life.
The kind of grace that I will send
will overpower your hardened heart.
I advise you to buy gold from Me
that has been refined,
before I refine My gold (you)
in the fire of judgment
designed to change you.
Come to Me now.
I am waiting.

*Now is the time.*
*This season was My final call -*
*My bridal call.*
*Do not turn from Me again,*
*or My eyes of judgment*
*will turn toward your life,*
*for your good*
*and the glory of My Son,*
*Jesus.*

Bible Correlations

*Mal. 3:2-5a;*
*Rom. 2:5,6;   2 Ti 3:2-5a;   Rev. 3:18*

Why is it that we so often need to be afflicted in order to consent to being changed?  If only we could respond  when, as the scripture says, His kindness leads us to repentance.

I believe the key lies in getting to know our God, and coming into an understanding of Who Jesus really is.  If we don't really know Who Jesus is, how  can  we even know what we ought to be like?  The more we know Who He is, the clearer it becomes Who He isn't.  With Him as our example, we begin to see those things in us which are not acceptable - things we just didn't consider all that serious before they were exposed by God's Truth, Jesus.

The world can't possibly see Jesus if they see only us.  "Lord, please draw us.  We can only pursue a relationship with You  and choose Your ways over our ways by Your grace - whether it be through kindness or affliction."

## FROM OUR FATHER'S HEART (C3)
### From page A39 in "A White Stone Workbook"

Do you hear it?
Do you hear the call
that stops My life from totally eliminating your life?
You have called yourself by My Name for some time.
Now I desire for you to look,
act and truly be like Me
from your heart.
Submit to Me
and I will change you.

Bible Correlations

Rom. 3:23-24;
1 Pe. 2:19-21 amp;   1 John 2:6 amp

Satan knows that he can't make most of us sin deep sins any more. If we are truly our Lord's, each trait that resembles the world falls aside as we continually submit and repent each time it is exposed to us. A greater danger to our witness are the less obvious, but extremly deadly character traits of self-righteousness, spiritual pride and the desire to dominate others or all of our circumstances. These traits, left unchecked, will destroy even the greatest witness.

The young in the Lord have a particular tendency to fall for this ploy of the enemy, especially those who are wounded before they come to the knowledge of Jesus. When they begin to heal, gain some semblance of knowledge of the Word and are accepted within the circles of Christendom, (especially as leaders of some kind,) they have a tendency to lose God's real perspective. They are marked by a modicum of success, but it can only go as far as they can propel it with their own knowledge, abilities, strength and personality. Only upon deep repentance can they move to the deeper things of God. Frankly, most become shipwrecked in a sea of need for earthly provisions, justifying that desire by calling it family responsibility or stewardship and minimizing their effectiveness to show a crucified life to others.

Someone once said that pride dies fifteen minutes after the body is cold. How alive is it in you?

## FROM OUR FATHER'S HEART (C4)
### From Page A34 of "A White Stone Workbook"

You, My people,
have destroyed My Name in the eyes of the world.
Your powerless prayers,
selfish lives,
self-serving gospel
and your disloyalty
have made you weak and powerless to represent Me.
My love for you
has allowed trials in your life to change you
so that you might become like My Son,
Jesus Christ.
I want you to be endued with His power.
I want to be able to trust you with My presence.
Why do you resist
the suffering
and the denial of your desires?
Why do you seek your own comfort
while others go without knowing Me?
How did your eyes become focused
on your own needs,
instead of on My desires?
You have denied My purposes,
My ways,
and have lost intimacy with Me in doing so.
Repent.
Turn now,
and We will walk together
in full accord.

## Bible Correlations

*Prov. 19:27;    Isa. 30:18 liv;    Isa. 58:6-7;
Hos. 13:6;    Hag. 1:4-5;
Rom. 10:14-15*

After a lengthy time of trial, it occurred to me that if I was going to focus all of my energies on simply surviving from day to day, I wasn't going to be of much use to God, or anyone else for that matter. It's far too easy to focus on ourselves, even when things are going fine. What makes it even more difficult to discern is that the attitude of self-focus has crept into the church and made itself at home. The standard in most churches is one of ease and comfort.

Our standard is supposed to be Jesus. If we would take an honest look at the Gospels, not picking and choosing parts that appeal to us, we would see a very interesting example to follow. Jesus did not lead a comfortable life. His life was only about His relationship with His Father and what His Father desired; not about how He could avoid suffering, misery, poverty, and any unpleasant circumstances. He had peace and comfort in knowing His Father and doing His will. Ours should be the same.

Now would be a good time to look at how much time we waste in the pursuit of our own comforts. How could that time be better spent to glorify our Lord? Repentance is a good place to begin, once we see those areas.

## FROM OUR FATHER'S HEART (C5)
### From page A23 of "A White Stone Workbook"

You are the righteousness of My Son,
Jesus Christ.
All that He is,
is being formed in you for My glory.
From the beginning,
I have planned all that is taking place throughout the world;
and each of you,
My children,
has a specific role for which to prepare.
Each task is very important to Me.
I ask you to persevere and prepare.
Submit to My work in you,
and My hand upon you,
as you are being developed for your part.
I am forming you.
I am changing you.
I am molding you to represent Me properly.
The plumb line of righteousness has been moved,
but not by Me.
It has been moved by your traditions,
doctrines
and personal habits.
I am, however,
bringing it back to My center in your life.
For too long,
what I consider to be a normal way of living
has been looked upon as extreme to many,
even in My church.

No more!
Normal is absolute purity,
devotion, dedication and zealous love.
It is a heart that is broken for those who are lost.
Normal is Our restored,
intimate fellowship
from which springs holy works,
allowing people to see My glory in you.
Normal is joyous self-sacrifice
and an ardent desire to be purged
from all unrighteousness
at any cost.
Normal is an eternal perspective
in all that you do
and on everyone that you meet.
You are being made normal again
so that I might be able to trust you with My Word
in all circumstances.
It is My great joy that you be excited,
encouraged
and at peace;
for I am at work
and aware of all of your needs.
Know that I am training you to live a normal life
as I perceive normality.
Your life will be a plumb line.
Those who choose My ways
will observe you and come to Me
because of how you live.
My Son showed you how to live a normal life,
and now I empower you to do it.
Devote yourself to Me.
I love you.

Bible Correlations

Rom. 9:20-21;   1 Cor. 11:1;
Col. 1:27;   Col. 3:2-3

I am reminded of the frog who was slowly boiled to death. If he had been thrown into a pot of already boiling water, he would've made an attempt to escape. However, he sat in a pot of water which gradually reached the boiling point. He never became aware of the danger, made no attempt to escape and died.

It seems as though this has happened to the church, as the ways of the world have infiltrated it. The plumb line has gradually shifted away from God's standards to man's perspective. Because it came gradually, one compromise at a time, we've failed to see how far we have drifted from God's intent and purposes.

God, however, knows the end as well as the beginning and everything in between. He has a plan that will come to pass. The only question is whether or not we will be an active part of it.

God's intent is for Jesus to be seen in every believer, so that the world might come to know and embrace Him before it is too late. Jesus will only be seen in those believers who have allowed Him to be the pattern for their lives.

Your choice is to decide whether you want to submit completely to God's plan and be an imitator of Jesus, or whether you want to continue to play dangerous games with God - games with an eternal impact.

## FROM OUR FATHER'S HEART (C6)
### From page A17 in "A White Stone Workbook"

Do you really believe what I have told you in My Word?
Do you understand how important it is to Me
that you submit to My Spirit
so that I might reveal truth to you?
Some of you have become so involved
in your own perceptions of My plans and purposes,
that you are weak, vulnerable and helpless to overcome.
Your life is useless in bringing others to Me.
The time is now to repent
and turn back to My true ways.
There is an absolute plumb line that I have established for you -
My Son,
Jesus Christ.
Become a study of Him by drawing close.
Go back to the basics.
Study the absolutes in My Word.
Be confident again of My sovereign power.
Be assured of My willingness
to draw near
and impart Myself to you
if you choose whole-heartedly to draw near to Me.
Start over.
Start fresh and pursue Me with the intensity of first love.
Abandon all outside,
worldly influences
and make My Son,
Jesus Christ,
your only love.
Come now, let's walk together.

## Bible Correlations

Amos 7:7-8;  1 Cor. 2:9-11;
2 Ti 2:15 amp;  Rev. 2:4

We live near a community in Wisconsin that has its own professional football team. It is a pretty good team at present, so much adulation is given to anyone involved with it. The players are on most TV stations with their own brand of "this," and proclaiming the graces of "that," in seemingly endless clamor. Some even have their own talk shows. Don't get me wrong. We enjoy what is going on as much as the next person. (Well, maybe not quite as much. There is not one foam cheese head in our house.)

Can you imagine how much credibility would be lost if one of the most popular players attempted to play a game of baseball on a game day instead of football? If he showed up in a baseball uniform, took some practice swings and seriously attempted to get in the game, how would his image be tarnished from that time on? His effectiveness to communicate his ideas would be nullified.

This ridiculous example is not so farfetched. In fact, it is played out each and every day by most of us in the body of Christ. We have been given a commission to present a crucified, holy life to the world, and we are showing up in a self-serving, prideful uniform. We even bring the bat of control along and swing it to show our strength. The world doesn't listen because we are playing the wrong game and have little power to do so. Our effectiveness to communicate Jesus is nullified.

## Section D

This next section is a group of "Father's Hearts" that have not been used in either "A White Stone" or the companion workbook. They were also given over a period of time since about 1982. He gave them to me at that time, knowing all along when they would be printed. How amazing! I am once again in awe of our Father in heaven as He reveals His timeless wisdom.

As I read over the contained writings, it thrills me to see new lessons each and every time. I am reminded again of the loaves and fishes story. The little boy presented a small offering, but it gave and gave until everyone was filled. On a much grander scale, God continues to give and give to us in so many ways.

Hopefully, you will find pleasure and new gifts each time you read the words contained in this section and throughout this book, time and time again, until you are filled to overflowing.

## FROM OUR FATHER'S HEART (D1)

My heart misses the interaction of love;
the love of a child
to His Father;
the love of a Father
that has everything
and willingly concedes to the needs that are of the child.
Not an indulgence,
but a willingness to share what is best.
I know what is best.
Have I not formed you from the beginning?
A time of fellowship is needed.
Draw close.
Do not be afraid.
I miss you.
Together
We shall explore the mysteries to you
that are knowledge to Me.
I am willing;
I am longing.
We have spent time
and now it is time
to go deeper.
I am willing to trust you.
Come and take of Me.
Come and let Me show you
the infinite majesty
that I have ordained.

Bible Correlations

Ps. 139:1-18;   Isa. 30:18;   Jer. 31:3-4;
Hos. 11:1-4&7-8;   Heb. 13:5b(amp)

I find it much easier to understand the love of the Father now that I've become a parent. As a parent, you want the best for your child. You have much to share and impart because you've already been where your child is going. You desire to spend time with your child simply because he or she is yours - a part of you. You enjoy seeing each discovery your child makes, and enjoy it even more when you see it become a part of your child's life. You have a desire to see your child come to maturity in all things and then see him or her go on to share and impart what they have learned. Isn't that just like the Father? How wonderful it is to have a real life example to help us understand how much He truly desires a relationship with us!

To those of you that may not have had the example of a loving, earthly father: Don't let Satan deprive you of the joy of knowing your real Father because of bad memories or weak examples. Father God is the epitome of a true and honest love. He cannot misuse or abandon those that are His. He will never leave you or fail you. Never!

Just for fun, get an amplified Bible and look up the verse Hebrews 13:5b. It is a promise to you. You can believe it, hang on to it and walk in it, healed of anything that the world may have done to you.

## FROM OUR FATHER'S HEART (D2)

*Hard times are coming soon,*
*very soon.*
*Prepare now.*
*Prepare.*
*I have been calling you to a deeper*
*and closer walk with Me,*
*to put aside time to spend with Me;*
*and still you neglect that time.*
*You go through your days*
*without spending time in My Word,*
*time in prayer*
*and in your secret prayer closets.*
*Unless you put aside that time with Me daily*
*and really get to know Me,*
*you will not be able to stand*
*in these last days.*

*Bible Correlations*

*Ps. 1:1-3;   Prov. 12:7;   SS 1:4;*
*Matt. 7:24-25;   Mark 6:31;*
*Jude 24-25*

Although we may have a personal relationship with God, and that means believing is seeing, why is it that we can so often adopt a "seeing is believing" attitude with the things of God? He has warned us time and again in His Word of things to come and has continuously wooed us to the prayer closet for our good; yet we very easily slip into the attitude most everyone had in the days of Noah. It doesn't dawn on us that we're functioning in "business as usual" mode, thinking that there's just all kinds of time available to us before Jesus comes back. Even those who thought the flood was a possibility did nothing to prepare for it while there was still time.

Why don't we prepare, even when we have some idea of what is coming in the future? Could it be that we are walking by sight and not by faith? It's difficult to prepare yourself when you don't see anything imminent on the horizon. But Jesus didn't say that it would be really obvious when the end was near. He said to be prepared because we don't know what day He's coming. It would make a whole lot of sense to prepare no matter what time frame remains simply because we would become who God desires us to be and accomplish what He has ordained for us. So, what's the solution? What would cause us to prepare for His coming?

Our option now is to keep on asking the Lord to draw us, and to respond as He moves upon our hearts. We must get to know Him so that we start to get a sense of the times and seasons in which we live and act accordingly. Our other option is trial by fire as the judgment of God comes down to accomplish what that quiet wooing did not. Which do you choose?

## FROM OUR FATHER'S HEART (D3)

*My children,*
*I love you very much*
*and I long for you to spend time with Me;*
*to know Me as never before.*
*Many of My children are walking in defeat*
*and are allowing the things of this world*
*to consume them*
*rather than the things of Me.*
*(I Cor 3:12-14)*
*I would say to you,*
*walk in My Spirit,*
*live by My Spirit,*
*and spend time with Me in My Word*
*and in your secret prayer closets.*
*You will be able to stand the storms of time*
*and all that is about to happen*
*on the face of this whole earth if you do so.*
*Put aside all other presumptions and plans*
*and seek Me for your daily provision.*
*Allow Me to be that provision for you.*

### Bible Correlations

Ps. 9:1;   Ps. 63:1;   Prov. 8:17;
Eze. 36:27;   Matt. 6:6;   Rom. 8:1-4;   1 Cor. 3:12-14

If you were going to go into battle and your enemy, numbered in the hundreds of thousands stood before you in full battle array, what would you do? What if, for some unknown reason, you had always thought that on the day of battle you would have to face such overpowering forces all alone. In your mind, from as far back as you could remember, you pictured yourself standing on this vast battlefield with nothing but whatever puny weapons you had in hand. Because the scene was played over and over for so many years, you had long ago given up any hope of victory. You knew that when the time would come, you were as good as defeated. It was simply a matter of going through the formality of losing big-time.

What if, however, when the actual day approached and you're standing there with the raging enemy before you just as you had pictured it, someone from outside of your frame of reference approached you with a big smile and a hearty handshake. Delighted that he had arrived in time, he told you to turn around and see what they had brought to help you. As you did, you saw a much larger, immensely better-equipped army, ready and poised for battle in your stead. What would you do? Would you turn down the assistance? Would you fight with them, knowing that you personally would probably get hurt or killed? Or would you graciously step aside and let them fight for you?

As obvious as the answer is, most of us have not made the right choice since we have met our Lord. We still take on the adversary, asking for whatever help that might be available, when we're not even supposed to be in the battle. We have really missed what Jesus has done for us.

## FROM OUR FATHER'S HEART (D4)

*Don't you understand?*
*All that is planned for you can only come to pass*
*as you spend time with Me.*
*How can spiritual well-being*
*come from physical provision?*
*Only Spirit can birth spirit.*
*Come to Me.*
*Hold the things of the Spirit close to your heart.*
*Let Me birth life out of the fertile soil of a pure,*
*dedicated heart –*
*a heart sold out to My Holy Spirit,*
*My ways.*
*As you draw near to Me,*
*I will show you truth.*
*Draw near now.*
*I love you.*

### Bible Correlations

Hos. 10:12;   Luke 8:5-15;
Rom. 2:4;   1 Cor. 2:14

I would like to tell you about my daughters. I would want to explain to you how wonderful they are and how much they have blessed me. If I had enough time, and you were interested enough to listen, eventually you would get a pretty good picture of who they were from my perspective.

Until you were able to spend time with them yourself, however, you would never have the slightest idea of who they really are. You would not be able to make a quality choice as to whether or not either one could be your friend.

In the same way, you need to learn how to spend time to really get to know Jesus. There is no way that you can begin to fulfill you promises to act as He would to the world, using other people's perspectives on Who He is. You could like Him very much, but you could never love Him enough to serve Him unconditionally. When times got rough, you wouldn't know Him well enough to do as He asks if your only knowledge of Him was the knowledge that I had given you.

I know that the above scenario is elementary, but it is the cornerstone of your belief. It is the key to the representation that each of us is to give to the world. That is what our life in Him is really all about, isn't it?

## FROM OUR FATHER'S HEART (D5)

*"My God, I choose to walk with You and You alone."*
*Let Me show you how...*
*Are you cleansed in the blood of My Son?*
*"Yes."*
*Have you chosen to lay everything down at My feet?*
*"Yes."*
*Do you desire only My presence?*
*"Father, I want to."*
*What stops you?*
*"My flesh is numb to the feelings of needing you."*
*Understand,*
*your flesh can't enter into fellowship with Me,*
*nor will it ever be able to.*
*Flesh and the world have no access to My presence.*
*Don't come to Me with what you see and know.*
*Come in, abandoned to the world.*
*Come to Me with helplessness,*
*clothed only in My Son,*
*Jesus.*
*I need nothing but your emptiness*
*and*
*commitment to His work on the cross,*
*not your own ability or works.*
*Stop being afraid of Me rejecting you.*
*I can't.*
*You are Mine.*

Bible Correlations

Rom. 8:5&8;   1 Cor. 1:29;
Gal. 3:3;   Heb. 4:16


The reasons that you or I would never have access to enjoy dinner with the Queen of England is the fact that, first of all, we have not been invited; and secondly, we don't have the credentials. Only those who have fulfilled whatever requirements it takes to get there will ever taste of the food that she might have to eat.

Our flesh will never be able to gain an audience with God. Flesh simply does not have the credentials to do so. Adam and Eve were removed from His presence as soon as the fleshly nature was able to control their decisions. Their reasoning ability separated them from the purpose for our creation in the first place - to be in a position where God is our God, and we are His devoted people.

Pride is the most distinguishable cause as to why we don't want to submit to His requirements, although ignorance and a myriad of other reasons stop us from going there. Fact is, we simply want to be in control of our lives. We want to be in charge and are unwilling to give that up, even if it means that we will never be in the true presence of Creator God. How foolish!

## FROM OUR FATHER'S HEART (D6)

*Do you understand mercy and grace?*
*They are continually flowing toward you*
*as you draw near to Me.*
*You may have as much of them as you need.*
*My supply is never-ending*
*to the heart that understands its need of them.*
*Always cleaning,*
*always forgiving,*
*they are living and active towards you*
*as*
*you empty yourself*
*and*
*desire only My presence.*
*I never empty of them towards you.*
*Take what you think that you need.*
*I will add all that is necessary.*
*You will never be without,*
*for I have promised them to you.*

## Bible Correlations

### Ps. 108:4;   Luke 1:50;   Jas. 4:6

Words can never convey the mercy and grace of God. You can read about them all you want, but they will remain words on a page. It's the experiencing of God's mercy and grace that bring them alive in our hearts. What a creative God we serve! Imagine inventing grace and mercy to draw people to Himself and to one another.

We need to be mindful of God's many acts of loving-kindness toward us. It's a great relationship builder. **Ask** Him to flood your mind and heart with those instances, and watch gratitude well up inside. There aren't enough hours in the day to recall His non-stop supply of them.

Thank You, Lord.

## FROM OUR FATHER'S HEART (D7)

You  have found favor
and are well known in heaven.
I take notice every time that you gather in fellowship.
Your prayers have been heard;
and according to My Word,
they will be accomplished.
I tell you,
My people,
that your labors have not been in vain.
They bring much pleasure to Me.
Keep sowing –
keep believing –
there will be much harvesting
both in this life
and so much more in the life to come.
At an already established time,
I will visit you in My glory.
I will fill you with My presence,
and you will know that,
truly,
My name is Faithful.
When I come,
I will accomplish what I have desired,
and what you have allowed to be sown in your hearts.
If you have allowed little,
you will,
in accordance with My Word,
see little accomplished.

But if you have hungered to know Me,
if you have thirsted after My Word,
if you have given yourself
to minister to Me
by what you do for others,
you will see the fullness of My pleasure manifested to you.
I reward those whom I treasure.
There is still time.
There is still grace for you, My people.
I so desire to fill every one of you.
There is work and blessing enough for all.
My plan for each of you is perfect.
My grace for each of you is sufficient.
Trust Me.
My name is Faithful.

## Bible Correlations

Matt. 18:20;   Matt. 25:37-40;   1 Cor. 1:9;
2 Cor. 4:16-18;   2 Cor. 9:6;   Gal. 6:9;
1 Th. 5:24 amp;   Heb. 11:6

If only we really believed God. If only we took Him at His Word. There is a children's song that goes like this: "My God is so great, so strong and so mighty, there's nothing my God cannot do." If only we could say and live that with the faith of a child.

As I read the corresponding Scriptures to this Father's Heart, I was impressed with how true, alive and active God's Word really is. I know we all say that, but how many of us really believe it? Do we believe that the Word of God really has a life of its own because God Himself has given it life to accomplish what He wishes it to accomplish? Do we believe that it lives to fulfill the wishes of God? That concept is foreign to us. Most of us put the idea of a living Word someplace on the shelf with those other "mysteries" of God.

In one of those "rhema" moments with God, I was shown by the Holy Spirit the reality of the living Word of God. It made me want to dig in, and soak in, and live and breathe the Word of God. It made me want to cry out to everyone, "Consume the Word of God. It is a living thing that can give you its life. It can affect your existence. You're missing so much if you ignore it. God has so much to give you, and so much for you to do if you will only surrender yourself to its application in your life. It is as important to you as breathing."

Jesus said that, "man does not live on bread alone, but on every word that comes from the mouth of God." I pray that the Lord will allow you to feed on the Scriptures; that they will nourish you, and that you will know them as He does.

## FROM OUR FATHER'S HEART (D8)

When was the last time that you wept at My altar?
When was the last time that you had
absolute abandonment for Me?
What will it take to be sold out to Me?
My heart breaks for those
that choose not to hear
and see the
times and seasons that they live in.
All that is happening around you
is so that you will need to come to your only place of safety.
I am your hiding place.
Listen.
Do you hear it?
That is the sound of the schemes of men crashing to the ground.
Look.
Do you see it?
Do you see the fear in the eyes
of those who have trusted
in the work of their own hands?
My Holy Place is a place of fullness in Me.
In that place with Me,
you are untouchable by anything that the world has to offer.
All of the din and death of the world cannot reach you
if you hold fast to My presence.
Come now! Learn to be in My presence.
I am a holy God, yes;
but I invite you.
You are Mine and I love you.
But you must come if you want to learn from Me.

Bible Correlations

Ps. 37:35-36;
Ps. 57:1;   Isa. 30:1-2;   Joel 2:17

*Why don't we just sell out to God? Why do we still hold back areas of our lives? We don't completely trust Him, do we? And why is that? It's because we don't really know Him, and the only way to know Him is to spend time with Him.*

*I'd like to tell you that there's an easier way than that - like riding the pastor's coat tails - but it just doesn't work that way. The pastor's walk was tailor-made for him. You need your own walk with the Lord if you're going to have an abundant life, a life only He can impart to you.*

*Consider the world and what it has to offer. If it's an extremely attractive place, more than likely your relationship with God has not developed much as yet. If it loses more of its glamor daily, more than likely you're pursuing God; and the more you pursue Him, the more you'll pursue Him!*

*Ask the Father to draw you to Himself. You can't pursue a relationship with Him in your own strength. It won't last. The Father is longing to reveal Himself to you. Find out what you've been missing. Call on Him. He's waiting for you.*

## FROM OUR FATHER'S HEART (D9)

*My child, much is to be done.*
*No more time for useless work,*
*no more time for play,*
*for now is the time to die to all that is of the flesh.*
*Understand that I will keep you.*
*Understand that My purposes will go forth.*
*You will be as a watchman*
*to many who are now scoffing at what is happening.*
*In a short time,*
*My miracles for you will unfold.*
*You will be amazed.*
*Walk with quickness and determination*
*as I open doors,*
*for much will happen fast.*
*I have told My people to prepare.*
*You must prepare for a time when no one has anything.*
*This preparation is not for yourself,*
*I will take care of you.*
*It is so that others may know what is happening around them*
*and come to Me.*
*You become ready now!*

*Bible Correlations*

*Gen. 50:20; Deut. 6:10-14amp.;*
*Isa. 21:6; 2 Pe. 3:3-4;*
*Rev. 3:8&10*

In 1906, on Azusa street, the Holy Spirit visited an upper room filled with turned over boxes and dusty discards. If I remember correctly, it was an old shoe factory loft. The impact of His visitation is bearing fruit even today. The power of God was strong enough to have sin laden people drop to their knees in repentance on the sidewalks two blocks from the room where a meeting was held. People that did make it into the meetings would lay under the rough benches for hours, crying and moaning for their sin and the offense that it was to God.

From that visitation, the Holy Spirit gave a warning to the church that would be living in the very end of time as we know it. He made three points to guard against and avoid.

He said that the endtime church would:
- have an emphasis on power,
rather than
on
righteousness.
- over-emphasize praising a God
that they no longer
prayed to.
- over-emphasize and concentrate
on the gifts of the Spirit,
rather than on the
Lordship of
Christ.

Have you looked around lately?????

## FROM OUR FATHER'S HEART (D10)

My child,
You have been longing to come to Me,
but I have so much more been longing
to give to you from the fullness of My love.
Come to Me.
We shall go forth hand-in-hand from this day on.
I shall be your God,
and you shall be My vessel that I can work through.
Do not fear,
for I shall become all in all in you.
As the enemy approaches,
stand fast in My provision
for I am the Almighty God.
I am El Shaddai.
I am the King of Kings,
the Almighty Conqueror.
Do not fear.
Do not lack in faith.
Just ask.
Just ask and I will be God to you.
My heart weeps and longs to be made God to My children,
for I have ordained it.
Where is the faith in this land?
Where are the cries for the sin that abounds?
Where are the sheep to be led?
A time is coming, is almost here, when no one shall come.
Do not tarry. Do not waste time, for I am coming with a mighty
rod. I am coming with the hand of wrath for those of disobedience.
Weep for them. Weep for them, and do not be one of them!

## Bible Correlations

Isa. 41: 10,13;   Isa. 59:16;
2Ti 2:21;   Rev. 2:26

As God continues to reveal your shortcomings, be of good cheer! God is doing the wonderful work in you that He promised. A while back, you didn't even know those things were part of you, did you?

I used to see everything I wasn't as a totally negative experience - probably my pride as much as anything else. Now, as the Lord gives me continual reminders of just exactly who I am, and how very far I have to go to be like Jesus; I am more able to give myself over to Him, knowing that only He can change me and that He desires to do so with all of His heart. My appreciation of Him has increased as He also builds the faith in me to believe that He really is Who He says He is.

Where would we be if God never exposed us for who we really are? Probably sitting comfortably in some church pew with no clue as to the rude awakening in store for us down the road. Have you seen any shortcomings lately?

## FROM OUR FATHER'S HEART (D11)

*Why do you not listen to My Spirit?*
*Why have you allowed*
*the carnal man in you to have his way,*
*so that you can no longer hear My voice?*
*I long to tell you of My ways,*
*so that you can be free.*
*Still, you listen to the logical,*
*the reasonable,*
*the perishing.*
*You must now turn from the ways of man,*
*and cling to that which is life for you.*
*My ways are not logical to the carnal mind.*
*Faith is the confident knowing,*
*when answers are not evident.*
*Walk where I tell you to walk.*
*See with My eyes.*
*Listen to and really hear My voice,*
*not the much louder voice of the world's logic.*
*The only way for you to be safe*
*is to listen to Me and learn My ways.*
*They are for you.*

## Bible Correlations

### Isa. 30: 15 & 18-21;   Matt.13:13&15;
### Heb. 11:1&6;   Rev. 3:22

If after you came to the Lord, He set you in the middle of a mine field and told you not to move unless He said that you could, how many steps would you take before asking His opinion as to where to walk? I would venture to guess that even the most ignorant of us would not move a muscle without His counsel. The dangers that the field ahead of us held, if we were normally foolish enough to move on our own, would deter us from being disobedient to His Words.

We have a problem. We will not listen to the instruction that our Lord has given us. Because the mines that are all around us are not evident to our carnal nature, we wander about unaware of the explosions that we are causing. We ourselves, and people all around us, are being wounded and some are even dying from schrapnel and flying debris. Since most of the damage is only evident in the spiritual realm, we go about our personal business causing untold havoc, and never even stop to wonder what all of the noise is about. Duh!

## FROM OUR FATHER'S HEART (D12)

*What is so sad*
*is that My people do not know where they stand.*
*They wallow in the mire,*
*when I have provided streets of gold.*
*Do they not know*
*that I cannot go back on My Word?*
*Do they not know*
*all that I have for them?*
*I am a thorough God.*
*Nothing I say will be missed.*
*Draw close.*

Bible Correlations

Ps. 119:89;   Isa. 43:13;   Gal. 5:1

A poverty stricken man had to travel to his job which was located in a distant city. Because he was so poor, and because it was the only job he could find, he had to make the trip there and back each day in an old, barely running rust bucket of a car. His livelyhood depended on that car. It was the only means for him to get there, even though it often broke down, causing him often to almost lose his employment.

So every morning long before anyone else was even up, the man packed all that he would need for the trip, and took off down the road in a cloud of smoke that would obscure him from sight the further he would go. Late at night, he would return exhausted, only to have to do the needed repairs on the car so that he could make the trip the next day.

One day, as the man pulled over on the side of the road to make some repairs so that he could continue on his journey, a kindly man in tattered clothes walked up to him, seemingly from nowhere.

"I've been watchin' ya make this trip every day. Been lookin' at ya from my porch over there," he said, pointing to a run-down shack just off the highway behind some trees. " I feel sorry for ya with this no-luck car that ya got, so I'd like to help ya," he continued. "In that barn over there," he turned and pointed to a barn that looked even worse than the house, " I got me this limo. It's yours if ya want it cuz I don't use it no more. I'll even drive ya wherever ya gotta go if ya want me to. Got nothin' better to do."

"Get away from me, old man," the traveler spat with impatience. "I have enough trouble without someone like you making promises that you can't keep." With that, he returned to the well-worn muffler to re-attach it.

The next day from his front porch, the kindly man sat and watched as the beat up jalopy hobbled its way down the road again. Shaking his head in sorrow for the embittered traveler, he headed toward the barn to polish the new limo he had inherited, wondering how he might use it to help someone that day.

## FROM OUR FATHER'S HEART (D13)

My people have need of Me.
They need Me now
as in the times of Israel in the desert.
Those who rely on Me for all,
I mean, all their needs,
will know Me;
not in the abstract,
but personally,
for I will reveal Myself to them.
However,
holiness is mandatory
for I will not abide in fullness
in a vessel used at times for unclean works.
Depart from your wicked ways.
Draw near to Me
and I will refine you into gold.

Bible Correlations

Mal. 3:3;  Matt. 15:18-20a;
Rom. 8:17-19;  1 Pe. 1:15-16

In the days of their desert travel, the Israelites were taught obedience by moving only when God allowed them to do so. They broke camp each time the cloud of smoke or the pillar of fire - which was the presence of God - moved. They stopped when it stopped. That is where they set up the next camp. They would stay for a short or a very long time, depending on when God chose to move next.

The generation that grew up under this kind of presence and mandatory obedience, knew what it was to follow God. They had known no other way, God allowed the generation that wouldn't obey Him to die off, so they were prepared to take the land that was to be theirs - a land full of milk and honey.

During their time in the desert, this people not only had a visible presence of God in the pillar of fire and in the cloud of smoke; they had his total provision, too. Clothing and sandals lasted forty years. Manna was available for them each morning and quail was provided once at their demand.

God has not changed. He is always the same. How is it then that we, the heirs of a better covenant, cannot and will not trust Him? He continually positions Himself so that we have opportunities to reach out to Him in our troubles, but we won't continue doing it. We reach to Him, not really believing that He is there for us. So we go about our business, stumbling and fumbling as the world watches, wondering who Jesus really is. What a shame!

## FROM OUR FATHER'S HEART (D14)

*The world
is again attempting to draw the line of contention.
They have categorized everything
into either political or moral issues
and have baited you My people
to submit to their categories.
Jesus did neither.
He did not become a part of any worldly categories.
He came to give dead people life.
Morality has nothing to do with Christianity.
Why should you fall into the trap of contention?
It is all vain attempts for temporary change.
Real change can only occur
when My Holy Spirit controls a life
and changes it for eternity.*

Bible Correlations

Zec. 7:13;   John 10:10;
John 11:25-26;   Rom. 6:11

One of the most effective tactics used by the enemy is to goad us into fighting battles on his terms. If he can involve us in physical battles of any kind, he has stopped us from being effective in the real battle, the battle for souls. Contention of any kind is Satan's territory. God is not there.

Before you jump on the very well-worn bandwagon of the need to protect others or to protect our rights, lets look at the life of Jesus. It would be safe to assume that He knew His Father's will and acted in a manner pleasing to Him, wouldn't it?

Jesus never dealt with moral issues except with the leaders of the church, who were leading people away from His teachings. Even that was really a spiritual matter. He never came against government, fought poverty, helped good causes or lifted a hand to protect the rights of people. He never fought to preserve anything of this earth. In fact, He proclaimed that all would pass away. When the zealots came to Him to help Him carry out a revolution that would set up His earthly Kingdom by overcoming those in power, they went away scratching their heads, mystified at His responses.

Jesus and His Father are only about the souls of mankind. Jesus' exclusive mindset was that of telling us to remove ourselves from any cause associated with the world's well-being. I would assume that since He and His Father were in full accord, we would be wise to follow Their thinking instead of falling for that old, overused trap of Satan. It's just time to "have at it" God's way, and do all that we do with the ultimate goal of the souls of people in mind. Jesus did; so would His bride.

## FROM OUR FATHER'S HEART (D15)

*Go after their souls aggressively*
*that they might be saved.*
*Give mercy,*
*show them Jesus,*
*lay your life*
*(your physical, emotional, spiritual life)*
*in your Father's hands as Jesus did.*
*There is no more time or place for pride,*
*self-worth*
*and*
*possessions.*
*Rob Satan of their souls.*
*Things are not as they appear to your eye*
*or as you hear them when people come against you.*
*Look past that so their souls might be saved.*
*Look through the circumstances to My glory.*
*How will I be glorified?*
*What spirit would I exhibit to overcome anything*
*that you may encounter if I were there personally?*
*What would Jesus do?*
*How can you present Jesus to them through that spirit?*
*Will you be a vessel of use in God's hands*
*as you lay down your life for them*
*as Jesus did?*
*Can I use you?*

## Bible Correlations

### Ps. 106:8;
### Isa. 6:8;   Phil. 1:8-11;   Jude 23

A while back, the Lord startled me while I was in one of those quiet, almost sleepy, could really be dozing kind of prayer times. His voice was quiet and full of love. He said, "I want you to know that I love your most aggressive enemies as much as I love you. There is no one on the face of this earth that I wish would perish. I want you to pray for all of those that hate Me. In fact, I want you to pray for anyone that will hate My children. Pray that they will be able to share My love." Then things got personally serious. "I want you to pray for those who will kill you. I don't mean that someone is going to do that necessarily, but I want you to have the heart that would care about their salvation more than you care about your own life."

By now, I was awake. Pray for someone that hated me enough to kill me! Love others - even the bad guys?

The Lord then reminded me of His actions on the cross. He had words of forgiveness for those who were spitting on Him and attitudes of great love for those who drove the nails in His hands. He told me to do the same to anyone that came against me.

It was enough to make me almost think that this life is not centered around my well-being. What a novel thought!

# FROM OUR FATHER'S HEART (D16)

Do not receive what you have not been given from Me.
Many voices that claim to be My voice will enter into your world.
They claim to be of Me,
but their true mission is to rob, to kill and to destroy.
Do not listen to them.
Do not give any place to them in your heart
or you will be confused and delayed.
In this season that you are going through,
I am cleansing, purifying
and separating you unto Myself.
It is typical of the enemy to misuse My Word
to stop you from being with Me and Me alone.
If he can do that
and you listen to what he says,
you will not be able to hear Me clearly.
Have I not called you to this time?
Remember when you heard Me clearly
to come aside and be with Me?
Have I not provided for all of your needs during this time?
Listen carefully!
Some cannot understand your life
because they are not ready to sell out themselves.
Some have been called aside time and time again,
but have refused.
I have given them their hearts' desire.
They are now blinded by the world and its treasures.
Some have refused My call
because of the fear of being out of control,
and they cannot trust Me completely with everything.

Others however,
the ones to be most pitied,
are those who have refused My call
and see their sin because of your life.
They will have no rest until they repent.
If you can truly live by My power and provision alone,
then they are made foolish by their own lives.
By your belief,
their unbelief is always before them.
They must either acknowledge their sin
or come against anyone whose life shows them their life
for what it really is –
only a shadow of what it could have been.
Pray for them,
but do not move to them in this time.
Their doubt and the spirit behind their lives
will cause you to become weak
and vulnerable to earthly wisdom.
I am not where they are,
so spend no time there
or with anyone who resides in that place.
It is a place of eventual spiritual death.
You come away!
Come away to Me
and you will taste of My life and My love.
I will empower you to continue in the times ahead.
I will show you My hidden manna.
It is only in the place to which I have called you.
That place is with Me
and Me alone.

## Bible Correlations

*Isa. 30:15; Jer. 6:16-19; John 10-10;*
*Acts 7:51; Eph. 4:27*

If you follow hard after God, you will be an outcast from most of the church. I'm not talking of doing weird things that discredit the integrity of the Gospel. I mean that if you follow the rules of the life of Jesus and move where He tells you, only when He tells you, people will not understand. You may find yourself giving away your home, taking a lesser job so that you can reach people, or - heaven forbid - trusting God completely for your provisions while you go into full time service.

One of the most heart-wrenching sights you'll ever see is the emptiness in the eyes of someone who has not responded to the call of God either because of fear or because of their lusts for the worldly goods they desire. Those desires may be simple things such as security, new clothes or a new car. They understand deep down that they have heard the call of their Creator and have said "no" when asked to fulfill the reason why they were born. Nothing, absolutely nothing, will satisfy the emptiness of soul after that.

Most of them eventually find themselves feverishly working at some ministry or filling a myriad of church positions to cover up the emptiness. The end result is almost always an involvement with other weary, critical people who themselves are doing good works, attempting to make a difference of some sort to cover their pain, rather than following after God's real plan for their lives. How sad! How grievous to God.

## FROM OUR FATHER'S HEART (D17)

*Do you understand how involved I desire to be in your life?*
*My plan from the beginning*
*was to be in complete fellowship*
*with the ones I have created and love.*
*All that has been done throughout history*
*has had one purpose in My eyes –*
*to bring those who will listen back into harmony*
*and fellowship with Me.*
*Why then do you –*
*who should know better,*
*who has been given eyes to see and ears to hear –*
*continue to doubt my love for you?*
*Why do you act as if I were not your Father*
*in the truest sense of the word?*
*Why do you walk in paths that you yourself have created,*
*instead of following My paths?*
*Time is very short.*
*Do not continue to be blinded and distracted*
*by those things that will minimize the importance*
*and nearness of My Son's return.*
*Cast off any thoughts,*
*deeds or plans that are not part*
*of My original plan for you.*
*Discover again what that is through My Word.*
*Re-focus your priorities by spending valuable,*
*intimate time with Me.*

*I will tell you My desires and plans for you.*
*I care about you more than you know.*
*The reason you do not know*
*is because you have been distracted.*
*Turn now.*
*Repent of your ways.*
*Come to Me and I will share My heart with you.*
*You need to walk closely*
*with Me again.*

Bible Correlations

Ps. 86:11,13;   Prov. 3:5-6;   Prov. 4:26-27;
Mark 6:31;   Rev. 2:17

I remember to this day an instance that occurred early in my Christian walk. I was talking to a friend of mine, someone who'd known the Lord a lot longer than I, and mentioned that maybe we could have lunch later in the week. She responded that she'd pray about it. After she left, I remember thinking, "She even prays about a luncheon date? That's a little severe." Deep down I just knew that God was going to speak to me about my reaction.

Yes, God does want to be intimately involved in the details of our lives. I still have lessons to learn in that area because I'm still guilty of setting appointments without giving it a thought as to where the Lord might need me to be at that time. Through grace and mercy, I believe there are times that I'm exactly where He needs me to be, but what about the times I went one place and He had intended for me to be elsewhere? I'm not saying the grand scheme of things was disrupted, but I missed the opportunity to join God in what He wanted to accomplish. It also shows a heart that's still prone to "do its own thing," that's distracted from following what is truly important - intimacy with the Lord.

"Lord, you know the pull that this world has on us. You know how quick we can be to follow its call. Help us to rise above it, and renew ourselves daily through Your Word and through time spent in Your presence. We love you. Please forgive us."

## FROM OUR FATHER'S HEART (D18)

*In the coming holocaust,*
*I will again be establishing "cities of refuge"*
*for the safety of those I know,*
*and all who have taken the time to know Me.*
*These spiritual "cities"*
*will be the havens of rest,*
*provision*
*and safety*
*for My bride for the season of change before My return.*
*Unseen walls of protection,*
*holy nourishment*
*and sweet refreshing will be available*
*to those who have learned to feed on the Real Source of Life.*
*My Holy Spirit will guide My chosen children*
*to these places*
*in the times of critical need.*
*Do not limit Me by your limited understanding*
*of what I am saying.*
*Go to My Word.*
*I have confused the enemies of My people*
*so that they might escape.*
*I have blinded the eyes of the aggressors*
*so that "paths" of safety might be found.*
*I have opened the eyes of My people to heavenly warriors*
*so that they might see the heavenly*
*warriors present to do battle for them;*
*alliances much stronger*
*than any foe.*

Nothing is too hard for Me.
Safety is not in where you are
but in whom you are with.
When you are truly with Me,
nothing
and no one
can touch what I call sacred.
Come to Me.
I am your place of safety,
your ever-present
"City of Refuge"
forever more.

Bible Correlations

Ps. 9:9-10;   Ps. 46:1;   Ps. 62:5-8;   Zec. 2:5

Thank God for His Word!  Without it, much of what God does and Who He is would be a mystery to us.  Isn't it a whole lot easier to reach an unknown destination with a map, build a house with a blueprint or assemble a bicycle with directions?  (Otherwise it would be, "What are we doing in New Hampshire?," "Why is there a picture window in the bathroom?" and "Daddy, what are those two bolts doing on the floor?" CRASH!)

I believe we're coming upon a time unlike any other. I don't know what it will all entail, but I am so grateful to have the Word of God and its history of God's dealings with His people. Knowing how God supernaturally worked in the past is preparing us for future supernatural occurrences. Although it may not all be understood at this point, the glimpse of the future the Word gives us now will become clear as history unfolds.

How important it is that the Word of God becomes a part of us. Much will be happening in the endtimes and not all of it will be the workings of God. How can we expect to know our course unless we know the One Who mapped it out for us? We need time alone with Him, so that He might reveal Himself and His Word - our very lives, and the lives of others, depend on it.

## FROM OUR FATHER'S HEART (D19)

*I am not interested in your good works.*
*All that you do in the flesh*
*is soon to blow away*
*as the chaff does in the farmer's field.*
*Only the pure wheat*
*from the finest seed*
*will be used to feed the multitude.*
*When will you come to Me?*
*What will it take to bring your heart*
*to the place where I can use it?*
*Don't you see that you have become so hardened to My voice*
*that I can no longer move you?*
*My will for you is purity of spirit,*
*mind and motive.*
*My place for you is with Me.*
*When will you come?*
*When will you choose the quiet place with Me*
*over the din of activity?*
*What will it take to bend your knees*
*and still your heart*
*that you might receive My presence?*
*Turn to Me now.*
*Doing good things for Me*
*in place of spending time with Me*
*achieves nothing.*
*Stop your activity.*
*Listen to My call.*
*I am waiting for you.*

## Bible Correlations

### 1 Sam. 15:22;   Isa. 33:5,6,10,15 &16;
### 1 Cor. 3:11-15

In my earlier years of walking with the Lord, I used to feel somewhat tormented as I listened to various sources tell me what I should be doing as a Christian. "You need to pray." "You need to witness." "You need to stop this." "You need to tithe." "You need to get involved in this." All of it was well and good, but until the Lord had the time to instill Himself in me and show me how things applied to me specifically - or maybe even show me that it wasn't something with which I should concern myself - I wondered how in the world I could ever be a Christian.

I think the problem was that I was trying to get a list together which would give me an outline of what I was supposed to do to become a Christian - which in and of itself would not help me one bit in becoming anything on that list. It's as if I said: "Here, if I do all these things, then everything's OK between God and me."

It wasn't until I started to learn how to wait on God, how to spend time in His Word and how to spend time in His presence, that I started to become and do the things on that list (some of them were crossed off) - His way. That's the key. We can do all the "right stuff," look like a man or woman of God and follow the list; and still miss God because we don't give Him time to deal with our hearts. Jesus labeled people like that "white-washed sepulchres," looking great on the outside and being rotten and decayed on the inside. That will work on man, but God is not fooled. In fact, He's greatly saddened because we will have missed the point and are in for quite a shock when we stand before His judgment throne. It will all go up in smoke.

Society, and even the church, are so activity prone that little value is placed on a life that is called to simply wait on God. "You can't just pray. How will your needs be met? How will you reach people for God? How can you give up what you're doing; it's going so well?"

Why not ask some people who took a step of faith and simply locked themselves up with God when He called them. You might start with the New Testament. Let's see. There's Peter, John, Mary Magdalene, Paul...

## FROM OUR FATHER'S HEART (D20)

*The last call is coming to My people.*
*I call and no one hears.*
*Hope for the lost*
*is nonexistent*
*in the minds of the dry remnant.*
*Caring for My desires*
*is nonexistent*
*in those whom I have entrusted with My Word.*
*Fear of Me*
*is far from the minds*
*of those who consume My grace upon their sinful lives.*
*No more.*
*I am the Almighty God.*
*Repent.*
*Return to your first love, My people.*
*You are cold.*
*You are empty.*
*You are trying to replace My presence*
*with the works that make you feel worthy.*
*Those works only serve your inner fears and needs,*
*not My purposes.*
*Repent.*
*Return to your first love.*
*Seek Me and live.*

Bible Correlations

Neh. 9:7-8;   Luke 16:10-11;
Luke 19:17;   Rev. 2:2-5

There is a familiar story about an individual who belonged to a small church. Several years previously, he had experienced a dramatic conversion to Jesus Christ and had followed Him diligently ever since.

One day, he enthusiastically approached the pastor to inquire how he might best serve in the fledgling congregation. The only open position was one of being a greeter, which he gleefully accepted.

Every Sunday without fail for many years, this man greeted everyone that came to the church for services. The congregation grew, due greatly to the hearty, loving welcome people had received as visitors. This man's ministry had a big part in that growth.

After a time the man - now in charge of many greeters - grew disillusioned with his position and wanted a more important position in the church. When he was asked to remain as the head greeter, he felt that the church did not really appreciate him, so he left. Eventually he became disillusioned, and fell away from the Lord.

The first love qualities of service, unashamed love and child-like enthusiasm are the qualities of Jesus. When we lose them, we lose real life.

# FROM OUR FATHER'S HEART (D21)

*Who can withstand My indignation?*
*Who can endure My fierce anger?*
*Though I am a refuge in times of trouble,*
*I am about to pour out My wrath*
*on those in disobedience to Me.*
*My flood is about to become a torrent*
*to those who have chosen not to listen.*
*The crevices in the rocks that hide you*
*are the pathways of the rushing waters*
*that I will use to purify My people.*
*You will be washed away*
*if your stronghold is not chosen by Me.*
*Come to safety.*
*Come to Me.*
*Rid yourselves of your adultery.*
*The time is past for it to go unnoticed.*
*Your shame will be exposed for what it really is.*
*Works of flesh.*
*My ways are the only way.*
*Walk in them.*

### Bible Correlations

Num. 32:23;  Isa. 2:20-21;  Hos. 4:6-9,12;
Nahum 1:6-8;  Jas. 4:8-10 amp;
Rev. 6:15-17

In the last days, the Bible says that men's hearts will fail them for fear. It also says that men will cry out to the mountains and rocks to fall on them and hide them from the face of Almighty God.

In those times, it is said that whatever has been your god will be that which is used to destroy you. If you have served pride all of your life, then the pride that will not allow you to bend your knee to Jesus will destroy you. If hatred and anger were your gods, then cursing God Himself for the distress that He is causing will be a natural outflow from that kind of heart, etc., etc.

It is amazing to me how people interpret strong warnings about the endtimes, which I believe are just around the corner. Instead of accepting them as the love warnings that they are and heeding them, people tire of them and continue to serve the gods that they have served throughout their lives. It is almost as if a purposeful challenge is being sent back to God - a challenge for Him to actually prove that the things which He promised in His Word will happen. No one can conceive that a loving God would actually allow these things to occur.

Believe God. Please, believe God. His endtime scenario is a portrayal of real people, people very much like you and me - people who did not heed the strong warnings that were given a short time before the end. They were strong warnings very much like these, in times very much like these, to people very much like us.

## FROM OUR FATHER'S HEART (D22)

Watch.
Watch with Me.
Turn from the world,
for it is destined to fail.
Wisdom will no longer be sought by those who are in power.
They will seek after power,
fame
and riches.
Anyone or anything in the way will be eliminated –
so they think.
My ways will prevail.
I laugh at the supposed might
of the small men with big voices.
Casting long shadows does not change the size of a person.
It's just the perspective that a person has.
You should see things from My perspective.
I breathe and the winds change.
My world will obey all My wishes.
Watch.
The world and all its supposed wisdom and power
will be stilled
when I decide to move.
They laugh at Me.
I know it;
I see it.
If they only knew how poor and lacking they really are.
Who will tell them?
You will.
Do not be discouraged and afraid for I am with you.
Go tell them.

Bible Correlations

Ps. 2:4;   Ps. 96:10-13;   Prov. 19:21;
Isa. 49:13;   1 Cor. 1:19-20


We need a BIG picture of our God. We need to broaden our horizons on Who He is and what He can do. As our confidence in and understanding of God increases, the supposed might of this world will start to appear puny and laughable.

God's creation is a magnificent place to look for His vastness and might. All of nature obeys Him and responds to His command. All you need do is recall instances of earthquakes, floods, fires, storms, infestations, drought, weather patterns, etc., to rekindle an impression of His awesomeness.

The world has trivialized and minimized God with the term Mother Nature. They refuse to believe that Someone is in charge. It gives them an excuse not to bow their knee to their Creator. However, even if one chooses to ignore the supernatural, you cannot deny what is seen in nature. The evidence will not go away - at least not until the Lord removes it - so the only other option is to bury your head in the sand. What reasoning person could conclude that things just sort of happened on their own?

There's a song sung in Christian circles called "Shout to the Lord." One of its phrases, "Mountains bow down and the seas will roar at the sound of Your Name," thrills my heart every time I sing it. It reminds me once again how BIG God is. Ask Him for those reminders. They're wonderful faith builders.

## FROM OUR FATHER'S HEART (D23)

*Now is the time.*
*The trials and circumstances in your life*
*are designed to cause you to come*
*to the end of yourself*
*and to have you see your great need of Me*
*in every area of your life.*
*It is an act of love on My part.*
*You are being prepared for what lies ahead.*
*You must deal with the sin in your life,*
*and whatever else you cling to at present;*
*or it will cause you to fall later.*
*Because of the work that I am about to do on this earth,*
*you must be totally Mine.*
*Our hearts must beat as one heart,*
*or you will go the way of the Abiathar priesthood.*
*They ministered to the people devoid of My presence,*
*most of the time*
*never noticing that I was not with them.*
*I tell you again - the time is now.*
*The season is now.*
*If you could see what is ahead,*
*you would embrace this trial*
*as the act of love that it is.*

## Bible Correlations

Rom. 7:21-25;
Eph 3:16-19;   2 Th. 1:4-12;   1 Pe.1:6-12;
1 Pe. 4:12-19;   Rev. 3:10-12

Because most of us have come to Christ for our well-being, we fail to realize that we've entered into a relationship with a loving God who is determined to make us capable of proclaiming His Word to others. Knowing that our over-all well-being is taken care of because of the work of the cross and our surrender to it, He devises means to refine and strengthen us. That usually comes in the form of trials which are allowed to come our way. These trials become platforms for us to make choices, decide lordships, and renew commitments. They bring our newborn "inner being" closer and closer to Jesus, while allowing our old nature to be exposed for the rotting flesh that it really is.

Paul prayed for the inner being of his friends who were undergoing a time of heavy persecution. He prayed that they would be strengthened with "power and might by the power of the Holy Spirit," knowing that it was of paramount importance that the inner being held the believer up to face the trial without denying God.

How do you perceive the trials that you face? Do you wimp out? Don't misunderstand, there may be grave circumstances that you are facing; but are they causing you to forget why you are even being given the opportunity of taking breaths? Are you using them to allow your flesh to survive, or have you joined the battle with God to destroy that rotting corpse called your old nature, or "self."

# FROM OUR FATHER'S HEART (D24)

Don't cheat Me of My time with you.
You have been formed to have interaction with your God.
I have purposely done that so that We both can benefit.
I benefit,
for I am glorified in My creation.
You benefit,
for I can share My love.
Much is stolen and lost when We do not interact.
I have a plan for you,
and you can only know it as We share true intimacy.
You need to glorify Me to become complete.
You have been made complete in Me
and lose more than you know
if Our time together
is not important to you.

Bible Correlations

Ex. 25:22;  Isa. 43:7;
Matt. 23:27;  Gal. 4:19;  Col. 4:19

How silly would it be for the Air Force to keep their planes on the ground, never allowing them to be flown? Pilots would be restricted to driving the planes on the ground, as you would drive a car, because no one believed that the wings were capable of sustaining all that weight in the air.

This scenario is foolish, isn't it? We all know that planes were designed to fly. On the ground, they can only go in a straight line effectively. They are clumsy, hard-to-handle, and bombs... well, you know. In the air, however, (where they were designed to be employed,) they function as the well built machines they really are.

So it is with us. We were designed to have interaction with our Father God. We were meant to pray, submit, praise, and worship. That is where we operate with optimum efficiency. These are not optional exercises or religious games. They are mandatory for us to function properly. Any other realm, any other function, and we become clumsy, dumb beasts taking up space - blindly groping for reasons to be alive. It really is that simple and that straight forward.

## FROM OUR FATHER'S HEART (D25)

When clouds cover the sky,
you make provision
because soon the weather will change.
When evening comes,
you bring a source of light
so that you can see.
When danger appears,
you call for help
so that you will not perish.
Listen carefully.
The clouds have come.
Make provision in Me.
The evening is here.
The source is Jesus.
The danger is soon to come!
Call upon Me now!


### Bible Correlations

Ps. 27:1;   Mic. 7:8;   Matt. 16:1-4;
Matt. 24:42-44;   John 12:35-36;   John 12:46


When I saw some previews for a movie that dealt with
tornadoes, I couldn't help but compare the preparations that the
people frantically pursued with the comatose attitude the church
has taken toward the imminent event of the coming of the Lord.

The horror that was portrayed was very real, as the coming storm bore down upon them. Knowing that they were in the path of devastation, all else was removed from their minds. The sole purpose for their every move was to find some form of shelter for themselves and their loved ones. Everything else had no meaning whatsoever.

It was interesting to note that all were brought to a place of level ground. There were no classifications of elite, poor or proud. There was no segment untouched by the upcoming event, just people grouped together in a common need. Granted, there were many varied ways of dealing with the catastrophe; but in general, there was no separation one from another. They all were affected.

Like any safety-threatening event, people somehow make it through. Time is a healer of all wounds; and we are a resilient breed, able to weather most storms that come our way. Quite possibly, that is why it is our nature to console ourselves with the "life goes on" attitude that pervades the church.

A startling revelation to some of us is that life will not go on as usual after the momentous event of Christ's return. Sure, there will be some people left; but things will not ever be the same. All life will be involved in catastrophic change, affecting outcomes for eternity.

Why don't we, as those who are supposed to lead others to that truth, energize ourselves as we would if something as puny as a tornaodo were coming our way? Maybe we don't really believe that it is soon to happen. Everything is ready. It is a promise of God. Wait! Maybe He doesn't mean what He says. That's gotta be it!

## FROM OUR FATHER'S HEART (D26)

*My children,*
*If you follow Me with all your heart –*
*if you really sell out to Me,*
*having no care for the things of this world –*
*you will be called peculiar,*
*even crazy*
*by those who cannot understand the things of the Spirit.*
*Even those people in dead,*
*cold churches will attempt to cool down your love for Me -*
*even kill it completely.*
*Shake yourself loose*
*from those who have attachments to this world,*
*even those who call themselves Mine.*
*Even if they will not give all of themselves to Me,*
*you be truly Mine.*
*You be holy.*
*You live to do only My will*
*and I will be pleased.*
*That is all that really matters.*

Bible Correlations

Deut. 14:2;   Mark 3:21;   Luke 18:22-24;
Col. 3: 2-10 & 12-17;   1 Pe. 2:9

The narrower your walk with the Lord becomes, the fewer people you will see alongside you. The world will cast you aside first. If you're following after the Lord, that isn't the worst thing in the world because you tend to become like the people with whom you associate. Remember, you're still in the world, (how else will they hear the good news of the Gospel?), but you're not of it.

Then it gets more difficult. Some in the church will decide that you've gone a little too far - you're a bit extreme, maybe even "legalistic" - so your circle of friends will shrink because if they continue to associate with you, they'll be forced out of their comfort zones. With time, you'll readjust. Besides, you're in terrific company. The Bible says that at one point, Jesus' friends thought He was out of His mind when He was simply going about His Father's business.

About the time you're wondering if you have any friends at all, the Lord will bring you in contact with people who are walking the same path you are. They may be people you haven't seen for awhile or brand new people that the Lord is knitting into your life for His purposes. You'll recognize them in your spirit as holy alliances. You'll see friendships from God's perspective.

No matter what part of the journey you're in, know that God knows best in the area of friendships, as well as in every other area. If there are friendships that cause you to feel unsettled, go to the Lord for His desires and counsel. Is that friendship there for God's reasons or for yours? If it's for God's reasons, then find out what they are and have peace in what He's working out. If it's for your reasons, then let go and allow Him to orchestrate His perfect plan.

## FROM OUR FATHER'S HEART (D27)

You do not understand
the concept of absolute authority or Lordship.
If you did,
you would serve Me for
My glory,
My honor
and
My purposes only.
You would willingly serve as Jesus did
no matter what the cost,
fair or unfair,
without question,
from your heart.
The coming times will teach absolute authority
to those of you who will not listen
and respond now.
You need to submit to My call to complete surrender.
Soon,
through pressures, persecution and heavy-handed rule,
you will learn that to which I am lovingly calling you
during these times of peace and safety.
Then,
your rights and comforts will be taken from you,
so that you can learn and choose the true heart of Jesus.
Obedience is an absolute in My eyes.
It always has been.
Learn it from Me in love and gentleness as I call you now,
or learn it then
from
My vessels who hate Me.

## Bible Correlations

1 Chron. 21:13;   John 4:34;   John 17:1& 4;
Gal. 4:9;   Heb. 12:21


Paul says that, at times, he is as if in birth pangs for those who don't know Jesus. He confirms that he will remain there until Christ is formed in them. He also relates that it is not the first time that he has been under the same burden.

I see that kind of heart as the same heart that took Jesus to the cross. Anyone that would carry the salvation of others so deeply and grievously, has no room for thinking of himself and his own well-being. It's very much like the time that Jesus sweat blood in the Garden just before He died for us.

I once knew a very caring individual who was called to move to deep intercession for the salvations of others. There was a precise season where the call was so evident, that each time she prayed, all she could do was ache and grieve for others. She said that the pain she experienced was akin to giving birth. The reality of those going to hell was so intense that she would weep for them for hours.

After a while, she cried out to the Lord to take the burden away. The pain was too much for her. The price was too great.

She was not willing to pay the price for walking as Jesus did. She turned down her calling, as most of us have when we care for ourselves more than for others. God is in the business of knowing how to get us to choose what He knows is best for us; that for which we have been created. He is good at bringing us to the point of saying " yes." Maybe it is a good idea to say "yes" in the beginning.

## FROM OUR FATHER'S HEART (D28)

Praise Me –
My life flows into the lives of those who praise Me.
Unbounded wealth is available as We unite.
I love to draw near to you
and I feel welcome
and very close as you praise.
I will never intrude on anyone,
but I delight
in being invited.
Invite Me –
Let Me dine with you;
it will be a joyous time.
I have much to share.
Allow Me to flow in the spirit that I have given you.
Living water shall burst forth.
In fact,
you will not be able to contain all that I desire to give you.
Come close to Me and receive.
Start now by praising,
for I am waiting for you
to open up to Me.


Bible Correlations

Ps. 63:1-5;   Ps.84:1-4;   Mal. 3:10;
John 7:37-38;   Rev. 3:20

Praise opens our spirits up to God. No wonder He desires our praises. He is seeking intimacy with us, longing to impart Himself to those He loves. In the Old Testament, we learn that God inhabits the praises of His people. In the New Testament, we find that God inhabits us! Through His Holy Spirit, He invites us to draw close, and at the same time draws close to us as we sing our love songs to Him.

Ideally, praise will be a natural outflowing of our relationship with the Lord. If we love Him, what would be more natural than expressing that love to Him through our praises. He also desires to express Himself to us as we praise, whether that be through His presence or as a reminder of Who He is as we concentrate on the words that pour forth from our lips.

What about those times when we just don't have it in us to express our love to the Lord? There's nothing wrong with a sacrifice of praise, because God is worthy no matter how we're feeling. He's a great fan of obedience as well as praise. Our feelings should never be the evaluator. They're unreliable. It's much better to have an honest heart before God whether the feelings are there or not, than to have an emotional release during praise and worship with sin harbored in the heart.

The Lord would love to hear from you. I'm sure you've got a love song in there somewhere. Why not let it flow forth? It would so touch His heart!

## FROM OUR FATHER'S HEART (D29)

My love is in the hidden softness of a quiet spirit -
the peace of resting before
a brilliant sunset
after a day of hard work.
Allow Me to be that quiet for you.
Draw near to Me.
Do not let the turmoil of your situation
drive you to a place
where I cannot touch your heart.
Do not let others determine how you will seek Me.
Rise above the situation in Me.
My Spirit is peaceful –
Draw near to Me.
My Spirit
does not move at circumstances,
but in wisdom
and knowledge
of what is best overall.
I know the beginning from the end.
Allow Me to determine the workings of your life,
not you or others.
My will is pure, not divided by self-motives.
I desire what is best for you.
Draw close.

## Bible Correlations

Ps. 46:1-6;   Ps. 46:10a;   Prov. 3:5-6;
Prov. 9:10;   Isa. 30:15;
Isa. 46:9-10


To allow the One Who created us to determine the workings of our lives is the wisest stance any one of us could take. It is fascinating how much power and control this world flaunts to show itself strong. We have all become desensitized to the bombardment of propaganda that would stop us from submitting to God in all that we do. Personal strength, winning at all costs, self-motivation, self-esteem. These are terms that are so familiar that we don't recognize them for what they really are. They are Satan's ploys to nullify the Word of God in which submission, repentance, humility and servanthood are keys to God's plan for real strength.

History shows that any nation that is preoccupied with sports and recreation is doomed to soon fail. It makes sense. Nations rise when people join together for a common good, thinking of others. Nations fail when there is no real glue to join people together. That is when people think about themselves, and that is when they fail.

God's plan for real strength includes the absence of self in any equation. His plan is the answer for all people. He made them; He knows what is best for them.

## FROM OUR FATHER'S HEART (D30)

*I am separating the wheat from the chaff.*
*I am testing those who have determined to serve Me.*
*Understand that I need to know*
*whom I can trust*
*to carry out My will in all circumstances.*
*No matter what the present may look like,*
*do not be moved by what you see.*
*My ways are not your ways.*
*When you have done all,*
*stand*
*and let Me create the next move.*
*It may not look as though anything is being done,*
*but I do not work in the flesh.*
*My work is done in the Spirit.*
*While there is no evidence of change,*
*hearts are being softened,*
*spirits are becoming receptive to My purposes.*
*Great armies*
*are being maneuvered*
*to establish My Word to go forth.*
*Oh, yes!*
*Much is being done.*
*Stand.*
*Be still and know that I am God.*

## Bible Correlations

*2 Chron. 16:9;   2 Chron. 20:17;   Isa. 55:8-9;*
*Zech. 4:6;   Eph. 6:13*


Sometimes, the hardest thing in the world is to wait. We tend to look upon waiting on God as doing absolutely nothing, but it is far from that. Living in an "instant" society, we've grown accustomed to having things on an immediate basis. What we often fail to realize is that God is very active during this waiting time, and He is making changes in us and around us and in connection with us while we are seemingly doing nothing but praying and pursuing Him. We waste more time running around doing unnecessary things because we have not learned how to actively wait on God.

During these times, do we find a cave, sit on the ground and contemplate the meaning of life? More than likely not. You'll be doing many "daily" things, but your spirit will be in a state of expectancy as you allow God to orchestrate all things as only He can.

When you have done all you know to do, why would you then do more? Has that ever really worked out well in the past? No matter what anyone else tells you, when the Lord says, "STAND," then you stand and expect and behold what He has accomplished.

## FROM OUR FATHER'S HEART (D31)

*The world as you know it is passing away,*
*just as I said that it would.*
*Satanic manifestations,*
*which will cause the mind that is unskilled*
*in the knowledge of Me to be confused*
*and reduced to a state of panic,*
*are about to take place.*
*You, however,*
*should not be surprised*
*by the powerful deceptions all around you.*
*You should even be able*
*to grow in intimacy with Me*
*through the most cunning presentations*
*by Our mutual foes.*
*Remember that we do not fight against flesh and blood.*
*Our battles are initiated in the heavenlies.*
*They are fought*
*and won there against spiritual wickedness.*
*There will be no time to believe what your eyes see,*
*or what your mind tells you.*
*If you look to what appears to be,*
*instead of to what really is*
*and to what My Word says,*
*you will be confused and vulnerable.*
*Even My elect –*
*those who haven't listened*
*to the many calls to intimacy with Me –*
*will fall for the upcoming supernatural manifestations.*
*Think of it!*

*How masterful*
*must the deception be to fool My people,*
*My children?*
*What kind of power will it take*
*for those who know Me*
*to serve those*
*that call themselves god?*
*Do not fall for cleverly invented trickery*
*designed to nullify the truth of My Word.*
*Come to Me while there is still time.*
*Solidify your faith now*
*or you will be deceived.*

Bible Correlations

Matt. 24:24;
1 Cor. 5:7;   Eph. 6:12;   2 Pe. 3:17-18;
1 John 4:1-4

The most fascinating, and at the same time horrendous thing about deception is its insidiousness. I apologize for sending a two dollar word your way, but it makes the point so well. The word "insidious" has several definitions - awaiting a chance to entrap; harmful but enticing; having a gradual and cumulative effect; and developing so gradually as to be well established before becoming apparent.

Satan is no fool. Without God on our side, we are no match for him. Deception is a major weapon in his hands and all you need to do is look around you to see how well it's working - and that's in regard to what you can see. Don't be fooled; you are not invulnerable. I believe one of the enemy's tactics is to throw a blatant deception your way, which you catch; and then sneak an imperceptible (extremely slight, gradual or subtle) one through the back door.

It is only the grace of God and His keeping power that saves us from deception. Yes, we must know our God and His Word intimately, but we must also have childlike faith that He will reveal the deception to us - sometimes before and sometimes after the fact, depending on what He wants to teach us. It's our only hope.

## FROM OUR FATHER'S HEART (D32)

*If you really knew
how much I love you,
you would never fear again.
The problem is that you don't believe what I say.
You don't even believe My Word.
You would rather believe the lies of the enemy of your soul
and the prince of this world,
than the One
Who made you.
Could it be possible that you could be believing a lie?
Have you been wrong all of this time?
Maybe it's time for you to change your allegiance
and begin to take My Word as your only source of truth.
I would really like that.
It would make Me very happy
to see you walk
in the power
and authority
that I intend for you.
Come,
let's walk together,
defeat your enemies
and bring souls to freedom.
I am always with you.
You can believe that!*

## Bible Correlations

Josh. 1:8-9;  Jer. 1:5-12;  Matt. 4:4;
Mark 7:13;  John 17:15-17;  2 Ti. 1:7;
1 John 4:18

     The meek will inherit the earth. Those who mourn will be comforted. The kingdom of God belongs to the poor in spirit. Those who hunger and thirst for righteousness will be filled. Those who are merciful will receive mercy. Those who are pure in heart will see God. The peacemakers will be called sons of God. The kingdom of heaven belongs to those who are persecuted because of righteousness. We are the light of the world. Not everyone who says, "Lord, Lord" will enter the kingdom of heaven. God knows us so well, He even knows how many hairs we have on our heads. If we are weary and burdened, we can come to Jesus and He'll give us rest. Jesus' yoke is easy and His burden is light. If I try to save my life, I will lose it. All things are possible with God. Streams of living water will flow from within  anyone who believes in Jesus. We cannot bear fruit unless we abide in Jesus. God began a good work in us and will complete it. God has not given us a spirit of fear, but a spirit of love, power and self-discipline. God will never leave us, never forsake us. Let us rejoice in suffering for it produces perseverance, character and hope. I died with Christ; I no longer live and He now lives in me. There is no condemnation if you are in Christ Jesus. We are heirs of God and joint heirs with Jesus. Everything works for good if we love God and have been called by Him. No weapon formed against us can prosper. Nothing can separate us from God's love.  We are more than conquerors through Jesus. We have the mind of Christ. God's Spirit lives in us. We are Christ's ambassadors of reconciliation. God's grace is sufficient for us. When I am weak, Jesus is strong. God has given us the authority to overcome all the power of the enemy. He Who is in me is greater than he who is in the world.

Hmmmm. What if the Word of God really was our only source? Can you think of any reason why we need more than that? Less than that? Anything other than that? Let's leave it at that.

## FROM OUR FATHER'S HEART (D33)

My gifts to you
sometimes come in the form
of great trials and hardships.
I know that it is hard for you to see My love
in difficult circumstances,
but from the heavenly perspective
it is the greatest kind of love.
Look at it this way.
I know what you are about to face in this life.
I know where your weaknesses are,
and
I also know
where you are vulnerable to attack.
If I didn't strengthen you in those areas,
what kind of love would that be?
It would be no love at all,
very much like an uncaring friend.
Let Me assure you
that I am hovering over you
in the midst of each trial
to make sure that it is not too much for you to bear.
It needs to be strong enough to change you,
but it will not crush you.
Rest assured
that I am with you through it.
I love you.

## Bible Correlations

### 2 Cor. 4:7-11;
### 1 Pe. 1:6-7;   1 Pe. 4:12-13;   1 Pe. 5:10

Has anyone ever given  you a stomach exercise machine or a treadmill? Did you ever feel like throwing the diet book that keeps showing up in obvious places - like inside the kitchen cupboards or in the refrigerator - in the trash, or giving it to someone who really needs it?

At those times, we don't think about the possibilities of heart attacks that could be prevented or about the quality of life that is fast eluding us. All we can see is the horror of making some changes that will violate our comfort zone, and maybe even cause hurt in the process. The idea of calling these items "gifts" is opposed to our normal reasoning.

God, however, is the most magnanimous gift giver. He weaves circumstances, orchestrates events and  stimulates relationships that stir up our nests, and cause us to sometimes wiggle with discomfort.  All the time,  He is hovering over us, making sure that His plans for us prevail over our own desires.

In one particular instance, as I was assuring God that I had  sufficiently learned whatever lesson He was trying to teach me, promising Him that I would never do it again, (whatever "it" was,) I felt His reassuring presence. He calmly told me that all would soon pass (none too soon as far as I was concerned) and that everything would be better. It was, and one day I'll figure out what eternal lesson I learned.

## FROM OUR FATHER'S HEART (D34)

*Behold My Name;*
*uphold*
*My Word*
*and I will allow you to see Me.*
*If you do what I ask of you,*
*there will be no limit to our fellowship.*
*You shall know My heart,*
*My desires,*
*and*
*I shall fulfill yours.*
*Many are being called even now*
*to a total submission to Me*
*so that My endtime work will be accomplished.*
*Be a part of that calling.*
*I invite you to My throne room to hear of My plans,*
*to receive your part in them;*
*but it will cost you those things*
*that you may not bring with you.*
*You know what they are,*
*so rid yourself of them now;*
*renounce and turn from them.*
*My power will then keep them away.*
*You need an awe of Me again.*
*I will cause it to happen*
*so that you will know deep in your heart*
*Who I am.*

## Bible Correlations

*Ps. 33:8;   Heb. 10:31;   Rev. 15:4;   Rev. 19:11-16*

Have we collectively lost our fear and awe of God? I think so, otherwise we would be a vastly different church. Over the years, the world has crept in a little at a time, so gradually that we didn't even notice. Or maybe we did, but we became more comfortable when things relaxed. After all, now Christianity wasn't such a hard thing. "God loves me, He forgives me and I'm going to heaven. Isn't this fun?"

Isn't it wonderful that God devises means to get His people back on target? Isn't it equally wonderful that He has the ability to keep us there? That alone should inspire awe of God, because we know that we certainly aren't capable of walking with God in our own strength.

Although we may think so, God is not a hard taskmaster. It may appear so from our point of view, but He knows that obedience is a real key to intimacy with Him. Think about it. Why would God reveal Himself to a people He could not trust? Does that make any sense? Of course not. You wouldn't do that either. If God is going to share Himself and something as crucial as His endtime plans, He needs an obedient, loyal, trustworthy group of participants who have chosen to cast aside everything that keeps them from fully surrendering to their Lord.

If we come into fellowship with God, we gain the privilege of being privy to and active in Who He is and what He's going to be doing in what will no doubt be the most exciting time in history. And if that weren't enough, we will know Him so well that all our prayers will be answered because our thoughts and His will be the same. "Lord, we thank You that You have given us the power to change and the keeping power to remain changed."

## FROM OUR FATHER'S HEART (D35)

*Do you comprehend what has happened*
*when you choose*
*to put your hand in Mine?*
*We have become One through Jesus.*
*Your belief that He really is God,*
*your surrender to the truth*
*that He has risen and is alive with Me;*
*your seeking forgiveness for all your sins*
*has allowed you to become part of Me.*
*You have received My eternal Spirit*
*and It is now at work in you.*
*Oh! I know how many times you have failed.*
*I also know how many times*
*you are going to fall in the future.*
*But you see,*
*I knew that even before you came to Me.*
*Don't you see?*
*You have become a dwelling place*
*for the Spirit of Jesus glorified!*
*As you submit your lack to Me,*
*as you understand that you can't,*
*in your own strength,*
*accomplish anything;*
*you give away your carnal self*
*and allow Me to dwell in you.*
*Each time you allow Me to be Lord,*
*I become more and more*
*in you.*

Cease from striving.
I love you.
Allow Me to forgive you.
Allow Me to take your sins.
You couldn't change your desires before,
why would you think you can now?
Turn to Me
and allow Me
to let old things pass away;
and behold,
all things become new.

Bible Correlations

Ps. 73:23-26;   Isa. 43:18-19;
Matt. 11:28;   John 6:27;   John 14:6,7,10 & 20;
2 Cor. 5:17;   Eph. 3:14-20

OK, who gets the better deal here, God or us?  I know enough about me to know that it sure isn't God, at least not from any perspective I can see.  How many people would you allow into your life if you could already see all the times they would fail you down the road?  Still, God does it each time someone accepts Jesus as Savior and Lord.  Not only that, He offers us everything He is and all that He has.  As if that weren't enough, He asks us to quit trying to make something of ourselves and just let Him do it for us.  Where else could we admit our weaknesses, sins, inabilities and insufficiencies to get a "promotion?"  Why do we insist on clinging to this life?  What is so attractive about that old person we used to be?  We just don't get it, do we?

## FROM OUR FATHER'S HEART (D36)

*The more you are willing to lay down*
*your life,*
*your thoughts,*
*your desires,*
*your hopes and your dreams;*
*the more you recognize*
*and realize that the path I am leading you on*
*is not one that your flesh*
*or natural reasoning mind would choose.*
*Then you will know the joy of being acquainted with Me*
*in My sufferings,*
*and you will be made conformable unto My death.*
*Surrender - surrender all.*
*I'm asking for absolute surrender.*
*Do not hang on to anyone or anything.*
*Be as dead men to the things around you,*
*and you will become alive unto Me.*
*It is only as you die to yourself*
*and all the things around you*
*that I will be able to raise you up in power*
*and newness of life,*
*to accomplish and fulfill My plan*
*and purpose for your life.*
*No death,*
*no resurrection,*
*no power.*
*Set your heart to do My will -*
*not yours.*
*Stop fulfilling the lusts of the flesh.*

## Bible Correlations

John 4:34;   Rom. 6:11;   1 Cor. 2:9-10;
Phil. 3:10-11;   Heb. 12:2;   1 John 3:2

Jesus learned obedience through the things    that He suffered, meaning the times that He won over His flesh. Complete obedience means that one willingly and joyfully submits to someone other than himself.   Always. The heart of someone who is truly obedient thrives in doing another's will, and never, never desires to have his own will fulfilled. It is impossible to represent Jesus properly to the world unless we take on His heart. He was always obedient  In obedience to His Father's will, He lived, loved and moved as His Father desired.

In times of slavery, a slave became a servant when he willingly chose to serve rather than be set free. It is no different now with us as we learn to walk with God. When we cease from doing the right things because they are  right, and do them only  because we want bless our Lord, we have entered  into that little known realm of  true servanthood. Our joy cannot be complete as slaves. It will only be fulfilled as servants, when our greatest joy is to do our Father's will.

God cannot trust slaves - even very active, good ones. He can only trust servants. Which one are you?

## FROM OUR FATHER'S HEART (D37)

Patience is My way
of allowing you to seek Me with all your heart.
When it seems as though I may never move,
understand that I am orchestrating
many facets so that they are all in order.
Do not be worried as I am causing all to fall in line.
Meantime,
I am doing a great and mighty work in you.
I am building trust.
I am adjusting motives.
I am sometimes dealing with an impure heart.
This is happening to each one involved
in any given situation.
Be patient and grow.
See what I am doing in you
and
submit to it.
Understand that much other than what you can see
is being done.
Don't move ahead of Me,
but don't by any means stop doing
while you are waiting.
There are many ways in which you can serve Me
while the greater work in you
is being accomplished.
You may even see some day
how each seemingly unimportant task
may be the seed of a great work
and learning experience
in you.

I have no urgency in My Spirit;
why should you?
Am I your God or not?
Do you believe that I have you in My hand,
or don't you?
Have you given Me control of all areas of your life,
or have you decided
that you know some things better than I do?
I really do know all your needs.
I completely know your circumstances;
and while they are being orchestrated,
let's you and I enjoy fellowship.
Let's work together,
so that My Word can go forth.
Look for a need
and
fill it for Me.

## Bible Correlations

Isa. 64:8;   Luke 19:17;   Rom. 2:24;
Rom. 5:2-5;   Rom. 9:20-21;   1 Cor. 3:9;
Eph. 2:10;   Phil. 1:6;   Heb. 6:11-15;
Heb. 10:35-36;   2 Pe. 3:9

I love the last paragraph of this Father's Heart. When I read it, I feel a tiny giggle bubbling up inside of me. I can just see the Father approaching any one of His children and basically conveying, "Look, you can't do a thing about the circumstances you're in; but I can, and trust Me, I am doing something about them. In the meantime, let's just go somewhere and enjoy each other's company. I'm sure we'll find someone along the way who has need of us, too. By the way, what you're going through - you will treasure it in days to come."

I remember a periodic comment made by a dear pastor who is now enjoying the Lord's company face-to-face. He used to say, "There has never been an emergency meeting of the Trinity." If we could only remember that maybe we could stop setting them up down here. Is God trustworthy and all-powerful or not? Of course He is, so I guess that puts the ball back in our court.

"Lord, give us eyes to see, ears to hear, and a heart that has the ability to trust you completely!"

## FROM OUR FATHER'S HEART (D38)

*If I were to remove everything from you*
*that is your security,*
*would you feel that I had abandoned you?*
*What would people be able to say about Me*
*if their exposure as to Who I am*
*would be an encounter with you*
*during a time of testing and purifying?*
*How would you spend your days?*
*Would I alone be enough for you?*
*Would they see Me in you*
*and desire a relationship with Me because of you?*
*Would My Word be alive in your life,*
*full of power and purity?*
*You believe that you are strong in Me*
*because your world is relatively secure.*
*You even teach others your own perception of Me*
*that is partially based on your comfortable circumstances.*
*I am about to change that in My church.*
*I am about to shake all that removes Me as your primary focus.*
*I will destroy all of the hindrances*
*that do not allow Me to have all of you.*
*Be at peace.*
*For some of you, it is an answer to your prayers.*
*For others, it is a fulfillment of My promises*
*when you committed your life to Me.*
*The world can no longer hear about Me through you.*
*It has hardened its heart because you,*
*My people,*
*have not shown them the power of My crucified life.*
*Soon they will see Me because of what I will make of you.*

To those who are blind,
even in My church,
it will look as if great hardship
has been placed upon your life.
You will know, however,
that it is My mercy and love
that are refining you
and equipping you for what is ahead.
Do not shrink from My dealings with you.
Do not try to escape from My refiner's fire
that will allow you to purchase pure gold -
My gold for your life.
I am ushering in a season
where only surrendered vessels,
full of My true Spirit, will be effective.
No one will be touched by empty vessels that are void of Me.
You will receive My true Spirit in the crucible of suffering.
Be ready.
Be prepared.
Be submissive to My hand upon you.
I will train you
and give you My life
if you respond to My love.


Bible Correlations

Ps. 37:4-5;   Joel 2:28-32;   Mark 16:17-18;
John 10:4b-5;   Acts 16:26;   Rev. 9:20-21


We had the opportunity of having the Lord seemingly remove just about everything from us for two-and-a-half years - friendships, finances, ministry, sometimes even His presence. What were we going to do with that? We'd be the first to say that we spent a lot of the time simply surviving. If I could go back, that would be something I would like to have changed.

What impression did we make on those around us? It's hard to say because hardly anyone seemed to really want to talk about it. It probably didn't make any sense to most, and those that decided they "knew" what God was doing with us walked away. I don't think the world found our circumstances so strange, but the church did. (Isn't that interesting?)

Being relieved of most everything you're used to gives you the opportunity to ask yourself some valid questions. What is my picture of God, and is it accurate? What is suffering and how does God use it with those who are His? Those weren't the questions you thought I was talking about? Those aren't the questions the church usually asks itself.

The point I'm coming to is that we, as a body of believers, need to have an accurate picture of God and an accurate view on suffering, especially if we're going to share them. Being "blessed" continually is not an indicator that all is well, just as suffering is not necessarily an indicator that you're out of God's will. How can we help others deal with the things that happen in their lives in truth if we don't have the truth?

The life of the believer here on earth is a crucified life. God knows what it will take to accomplish that in each of us. Do we blow it along the way? Yes. God has taken that into account in His dealings with us. Keep going. God is in the business of putting an accurate picture of Himself in your life, not only for your sake, but for the sake of others. And isn't that an answer to your prayers?

"Lord, please don't take me out of the refiner's fire until your goals are accomplished." That's hard to pray, but so rewarding!

## Section E

### Introduction to "Early Morning Conversation"

The following "Early Morning Conversation" is probably one of the writings more dear to my heart than any other contained in this book. I don't believe that it is more significant than the others in any way - for I believe that almost any page contained in this book could be used by the Lord to help the reader  draw closer to the Him, which is why this book was written - but it stands out to me because of the way that it came about.

From 1987 to 1994, I had been given the privilege of operating a local radio station. The challenges to initiate and deliver the format that I was told to present to the listener were, at the time, unique and somewhat controversial in comparison to the other Christian stations in the area. In the early stages of programming, I was told often that a format of straight-forward proclamation of the need for repentance, combined with  high praise music, would never garner enough financial support to be able to continue. This, combined with the other challenges  of a small coverage  radio signal and the mandate of never allowing the raising of funds over the air, completed the sometimes seemingly "hopeless" picture.

In one of the many "valley" experiences, whereby the Lord was literally all that I had - for everyone and everything else seemed to say that there was no way I could continue another day -  the Lord moved in a particularly strong way. (Please understand that this time at the radio station, and especially during these "valley" times, was the most wonderful time in my life, in retrospect. I learned to become comfortable in desperately needing My Lord, which I believe to this day is the only way we truly get to know Him.)

As this particular morning developed, I found myself alone again with an intense need, crying out in my fear and worry and telling God how important it was for Him to move on my behalf. Instead of answering my petition in a manner that I considered reasonable, He chose to show me my real heart, and my true purpose for doing much of what I do. (As you know, that is usually what answered prayer looks like.)

He then reminded me of the "Father's Hearts" that were lying on my desk at the time, and had me page through them. As I did this, He would tell me to write down specific questions and fears in single statements on individual pieces of paper - one question or fear per piece of paper. Every so often, seemingly at random and without my reading it, He would have me place a "Father's Heart" after the page with the question on it. At the end, I had a stack of alternating pages with questions each followed by a "Father's Heart."

Please enjoy the outcome of this unique time.

( Please note that some portions of this section are found separately in other parts of this book.)

### Early Morning Conversation

#### "Yes, Lord?"

The last call is coming to My people. I call and no one hears. Hope for the lost is nonexistent in the minds of the dry remnant. Caring for My desires is nonexistent in those whom I have entrusted with My Word. Fear of Me is far from the minds of those who consume My grace upon their sinful lives.

No more. I am the Almighty God. Repent. Return to your first love, My people. You are cold. You are empty. You are trying to replace My presence with the works that make you feel worthy. Those works only serve your inner fears and needs, not My purposes. Repent. Return to your first love. Seek Me and live.

#### "But how do I start, Lord?"

Adjust your timetables to fall in line with Mine and you will be free. Your struggles, worries and concerns do not have a place in the life I have chosen for you.

Think on this. I am God – the one true God. I have all power – power far beyond your most intense imagination. You are My child through your acceptance of My Son, Jesus, and what He has done for you. Because of that, My life would flow freely to you if you would choose to accept it. That would mean that nothing could harm the eternal you. You could be free from all strife and worry simply by trusting that I care enough to take care of you.

Your life is not free only because you hinder Me. Satan is defeated. There is no hold over your life to stop you from receiving My presence. Why do you choose to believe the lies of the world that bind and condemn you instead of My Word that eternally works in you to set you free?

I love you. Choose to receive Me and My Word and you will be free.

> "But Lord, I am so weak.
> I have failed You so often."

My holding power is much more powerful than the sinning power of your flesh. When will you grasp the reality of what has been done on the cross for you? Its work runs deeper than any force. Its power is so much greater than anything that may attempt to come against it.

When Jesus died, all that hindered My presence from becoming active and available in your life was removed forever. When He arose, death itself was defeated. Think on that. What that means for you is the freedom to receive My life, My eternal life, and the wealth that comes to you by My presence being with you in your life forever.

When hardship comes, don't attempt to deal with it by your knowledge or ability. Apply My life to it. Wait for My presence to move. Rest in Me. See My work being done in all situations. Be free by My Spirit and you will have an abundance no matter what the outward circumstances might appear to be.

> "How is it that nothing seems to change? The world gets darker and I feel farther from You, more helpless, no matter what I do."

Holiness, denial of self, sacrifice and the crucified life. Why do you not seek them? They are the true path to happiness. You fight to protect those things you hold tight and call it My work.

You walk without power because you have not made Me your source of power. You are ineffective by My standards, but your search to fulfill your personal needs blinds you from seeing how barren your life really is. In doing your work and calling it Mine, you have become angry, fearful and in need of changing your world. How foolish. How vain.

I am seeking those who cherish holiness unto Me. I will use those who turn from the world and its ways. Despise those things which stop you from giving up your life completely to Me.

"But Lord, it seems that the things of the world
have such a hold on me,
not really bad things,
but things that distract me from really seeking You.
I feel so bound, so torn."

Holiness is freedom for you. When Jesus was with you on earth, He never set His mind on the things of the earth. My purposes and My goals were always His goals. As He kept His heart on things above, He walked through all earthly circumstances untouched. Even on the cross, He was untouched. There was no earthly power that put Him there. Schemes and dreams of mere men were of no effect, for He was not moved by them.

That same freedom is yours if you trust in Me. You need not be touched by that which is around you. Surrender fully to Me. Seek My purposes rather than your own. Learn of Me and My ways. Submit to My Spirit that you might be free. The work that I plan for you is for your best interest. Submit to it. You, too, can be untouchable if you keep your eyes on Me.

"But if I fully concentrate on You,
I look like a fool.
I can't just stop what I'm doing.
How will I live?
Surely You don't expect me to give up everything?"

When did I ever say that ease and comfort would be your lot? Look into My Word. Those that I called My own, those I held dear to My heart at times had no place to live. Even My own Son had no comforts of this world. You seek to satisfy your own needs and call it My will for you. I prosper you and you use it to pad your rest areas.

Do you not see that I cannot use you with a heart that has grown cold? The weight of your possessions and lusts and fears of loss have nullified your testimony. You look no different than the world.

Change your hearts now. Turn from seeking Me for your own gain. The selfless life is the life to which I have called you. You gave Me everything. Why do you take it back?

I want to use you for My purposes, but you are too busy serving your own needs. The people perish all around you and you don't even look up from your toil. You praise Me with your lips, but your hearts are far, far from Me. Return now, that I might use you.

"But I thought I was doing Your work.
I thought You told me to show the world its sin.
I am trying to be an example for You,
to bring people to You."

From My perspective, some of you are acting no differently than the world that is perishing. You are using its methods to *change its unchangeable heart. Why would you think that true, lasting change can be accomplished by the ways of man? Laws never change hearts, for the heart is wicked. When you move in the flesh, fleshly changes result.*

*I have never called you to pursue anything but Me. When you do that, we move in the spiritual realm to change hearts, to save those who are perishing. My Word shows how fallen man is helpless to even see the need to repent and change his ways. My Word shows how My covenant is invoked when My Spirit moves on the heart to come to repentance. When that happens, eternal changes result. That is My way. You cannot see, however, because you want changes your way and you are ineffective because I cannot be with you to empower you because it is not My way. It never will be.*

*I have one purpose for you now that you are Mine. It is the purpose that My Holy Spirit, Who is now in you, has always had. He has always proclaimed the beauty of Jesus to a world out of answers, a world dying in its sin. He has always moved so that those who are perishing might see, and come and be saved.*

*Why are you not moving in that same direction? All else that seems important is folly. I am not in it. Why would you be?*

"But I thought I was moving with You.
I'm involved.
I thought that was Your work."

*Where is the weeping at the altar? Where is the true denial of self? Where is the desire for a crucified life? How long do you think I should tarry? How long do you feel I should hold back My judgment?*

*I have called you and entrusted you with My Word, My light to your dying generation, and you have only served yourself.*

Soon your fleshly desires will be shown for the little value they really are. Buy from Me gold refined in the fire. Turn from your ways. They are far from My ways. Turn now. The time is short.

> "If that is true, Lord, what do we do?
> Where do we go?"

Your nation has turned its back on Me and you attempt to change it in your own strength. How foolish. Don't you see that I have given it over to its own sin that it might be consumed? I am not in its folly. Why should you be?

You, My people, have held abominable gods close to your heart. You have befriended the idols of the land. As I deal with your nation, you will be purged. You will be purified. There is still time for you to find safe harbor in Me. Rend your garments, weep for your sin. Turn from your idols. Stop useless activities to protect yourself. There is no protection other than Me.

Seek Me, for I am safety. Seek Me, for I am power. Seek Me, for I am the only stronghold for your children. Stop and think. If I have lifted My hand what could you do in your strength to change that? Open your eyes and see.

> "Oh, Lord. Show me what I need to do.
> Open my eyes that I might see.
> Create in me a clean heart
> and renew in me a right spirit.
> Show me.
> Change me as You promised.
> I feel helpless.
> I don't know how to change.
> I don't know where to start,
> or what to do.
> Help me."

Your carnal mind cannot begin to understand what I have planned for you. I call you My children, that you can understand. When My glory is manifested, My Word says that you will be as I am (I John 3:2.)

If you could only believe. If you would only come close enough that I might express Myself to you. Your eyes are big towards what is happening around you. In your disloyalty, the world is powerful. In your obedience, you can see a little more of My perspective. There is nothing too hard for Me. There is nothing to fear if you choose intimacy with Me over activity in the flesh. My plans for you – who you are now and what you shall become – do not depend on the world and its ways. They are not changed by loud voices.

Understand I do not change. I do not waver. I do not fail. My Word is true and at work even now in the din of life. To see My purposes, you must turn to Me. I don't mean for you to pray about things; I ask you to come to be changed.

I am not interested in what you do as much as I am interested in who you are becoming. How can old things pass away if you remain in them? You are no longer part of this world. Separate yourself from it, for it is soon passing away. Only My Word, My ways, will remain. Come to Me now. I love you.

"Yes, Lord."

# Section  F

## Exhortations section

## How to use this section

These exhortations are to be used in conjunction with your prayer time. They are written to be used as you would use the Psalms or Proverbs in the Bible, as they have no definite beginning or ending.

Some individuals simply read three or four lines and then go to the Bible as they are led. Others may read several pages before the Lord reveals what He may be trying to say to them at that moment.

As you read, enjoy how the Lord may direct you to benefit from them.

God
does not anoint
plans,
schemes
or
programs;
even
right sounding ones.

God anoints
men and women
who are sold out to Him
and
Him alone,
through Jesus.

The Christian walk
is in the life
of
men and women themselves-
not the works.

God
makes them
who they should be,
because
the messenger
is as important to God
as the message.

Any works
we do
must flow from a life
dedicated
to Christ.

It may take two years or two days
to complete a project,
but
it could take twenty years
for God
to prepare the person
for that same project.

To be effective,
each person in Christ's service
must submit
to the molding,
forming and shaping of his heart
so that it becomes like the Savior's –
dead to the world
and alive
only
to the things of God.

It is time to submit to the Father's hand,
then
relate His love
to those He is calling
for His service.

One
of the most
propelling forces
behind
the life-changing,
convicting
presentation of the Gospel
to the world
is
the energy of a life
of self-denial;
a life crucified,
joyfully
serving the Lord
for the best interests
of others.

Christians
cannot be hearers only
of the Word,
but doers.

We
should not develop
projects,
but pray
for
changed men and women.

God
does not need
great sermons or gifts,
but
people
of great faith,
holiness
and
love.

A life
lived in front of people,
learned
in fellowship
with God in secret,
can be used
by Him.

Begin now
to hear
the trumpet call
to
the life
desired by God.

It seems to be
more
important
to us as Christians
to learn
than it is
to submit to the One
Who has all knowledge.

Our pride of achievement
is diametrically opposed
to the act
of total submission
to God
for His purposes
in our lives.

We would sooner learn
about God
than learn from Him
while
being with Him.

The true Christian life
is one that is
God-ordained,
God-anointed, God-breathed
and
God-centered.

A true Christian
is one
whose heart
is single to the purposes
of God.

The flesh
and the world
have been nailed to the cross.

All reason for existing
is to allow
the life of Christ
to flow unto those in need.

Any provision
of self and worldly ways have,
through the power of God,
no effect nor bearing
on the actions
and responses
of mature Christians.

It is time to choose to grow
in the attributes of the One
Who has called us
to Himself.

*Our life
must be totally absent of self
and
exist for
and
because of God's will.*

*Unless
you understand
your thorough bankruptcy,
your total incapability,
your absolute helplessness
to live
the Christian life;
unless
you have cried out
from the depths of your heart,
understanding your moral
and
spiritual decay;
until
God Himself has filled you
with
His power,
His ability
and
His wealth,
you
can never truly serve Him
from
a
crucified heart.*

God
must rule
in
your
innermost being.

If
any part of you
still
has its way,
all that you do
will
fall short
of God's perfect will.

His
true anointing and power
cannot flow
through an uncrucified,
self-serving vessel.

Cry out to the Father
for a pure heart of service,
a heart
crucified to all
that
is not of God.

The
Christian life
will cost you everything –
death
to all that is of self,
crucifixion
to the things of this world,
and
the loss
of all
for the sake of finding Christ.

The
Holy Spirit
can move freely
through
the crucified Christian.

True life is imparted
as it flows unimpeded
through the temple
dedicated
to the sanctity
of God's life.

Self-esteem and personal ability
have no place
in the life
of
the person dedicated to God.

We
can only stumble
and
be confused
if
our own nature
is allowed place
in
communion with,
or
in the service of God.

All
provision, strength and capability
come from
and
are dedicated to God,
if
there is any value to their use.

Offer yourself
as
a temple to be sanctified,
so it is fit
for
the Father's presence.

*Any work*
*that has not been*
*received from,*
*ordained by*
*and dedicated to God*
*is doomed*
*to only temporary effectiveness*
*at best.*

*Eternal consequences*
*can only come*
*from the One Who is Eternal*
*through*
*a consecrated vessel.*

*Directions*
*from anyone*
*but God*
*may appear to be of value,*
*but*
*lack*
*the life-changing,*
*God-anointed power*
*that*
*comes from*
*God-breathed,*
*God-inspired,*
*God-empowered*
*actions.*

We
walk in fear
because we don't know our Father.

Our life
is ineffective
because
we strive to accomplish
our own idea of what God wants
in our own strength.

We
do works for God
from
a worried, striving heart.

Our life
should be at peace
and
thrive
from doing those things
that are of the living God,
received _from_ Him
in times of communion _with_ Him.

Seek to do God's work
His way,
in His strength and provision,
through
the Holy Spirit.

We,
as Christians,
are to be pitied
if what we do is not of God.

We
are no different than the world
if our works
are not
God-ordained,
God-breathed.

Except for the fact
that our hearts are seared by God
from the self-serving,
competitive edge and follow through
needed to bring a project to pass,
we
are the same as the world.

We
are truly to be pitied,
for we fit nowhere
when we use the world's ways
to accomplish
God's purposes.

We
are laughed at
and
pointed to as worthless;
held up by the world
as one more
second-rate mission,
inconsequential
in man's eyes
if
God
has not
breathed
His
presence
into
our lives.

Start living
only for that
which has
eternal consequences.

Choose
to separate from the world
and its ways,
and desire
to stand approved
of God.

A godly life
can only come
from
continual communion with God.

A lifetime
of
tapes,
programs,
studies,
sermons
and
literature about God
fall short
if they replace
intimate moments with God.

A Christian body
with second-hand knowledge
and
experience of our Savior
is ineffective to change hearts and lives.

Only out of personal interaction
with
a living God
can we even hope
to be
effective for Him.

Have
you spent
enough time
with the Father
through
Jesus?

If
you
haven't been
with your Lord
today,
go there now.

Turn
the world
off
and
resume the quest
when
you are refreshed
in Him.

Quiet,
intimate,
convicting moments.
Tearful heart interaction,
joyful spirit revitalization,
restful assurance
of one
who is loved.

These
are but a
small part
of those special times
with
the One
Who loves us most.

Guidance,
life direction,
answers,
hope
and
strength
come
as we listen
to
our Lord.

Praise,
worship,
an understanding
of His awesome wealth,
a wonder
of His matchless beauty
begin
as we press in.

Communion
of the beloved
and
the One Who is love
as we stay.

Replace
your worldly activities
with a commitment
to have fellowship
with your Heavenly Father.
As you do,
He promises
to impart Himself
to you.

*Why do you live where you do?*

*If you have been placed there*
*by God,*
*what would*
*His purposes be*
*for doing*
*that?*

*If you are where you are supposed to be,*
*what effect*
*are you having*
*on*
*your surroundings?*

*How many lives*
*are*
*changed*
*each month?*

*Do they even recognize you*
*as*
*being different?*

*Have*
*you prayed for your neighbors*
*individually,*
*collectively?*

Is
your life
a witness
of
God's love?

If not,
why not?


Father God,
please
raise up the heart
of
"Jesus with skin on"
in
each of us
to
eternally
affect the world.

Why
was Jesus tortured,
mocked, spit upon, nailed to a cross
and left to die?
Was it so you could live in comfort
while
the world around you goes to a literal hell?
If
Jesus were with you right now,
could you justify
your supposed needs
to Him,
or
do you think He would ask you
to change your focus?

Well,
He is with you right now.

The
resurrected Lord
that you, at one time,
vowed to serve with all your heart,
the One
you said you would give everything to,
is by your side,
waiting for you to live the life He did;
the life
that
you said
you would live.

You know
it's time
to
make some changes.

Go
to Him
now,
and
be set free
to
live for Him.

Please
don't be caught
holding
the
gold of the world
when
God asks
for the fruit
of the stewardship
with which
He
has
entrusted you.

Time
is very short.

You
need to stop focusing
on
your own needs and desires
and
begin to listen to our Lord
for
direction and purpose in your life.

It is no mistake
that
you have been born
into
times such as these.

You are being raised
in God's family
for a specific role to play,
a very important role
that fits into
the overall plan of God.

You must not take your part lightly.

God
does not make
mistakes.

He knows
who
and what you are,
and
is confident
that you will become
all
that you need to be.

Seek Him
with
diligence.

Understand
who you are in Jesus Christ,
and be confident
of
His promises to complete the work
He
has begun
in
you.

*You are  of great value!*

*It doesn't matter*
*what you've done*
*or*
*how many times*
*you've failed.*

*God*
*sees you with loving eyes*
*and has*
*arms open to your fellowship.*

*He*
*invites you*
*to come*
*and*
*spend time with Him.*

*When you do,*
*you will receive*
*all*
*of the fulfillment*
*that you have attempted*
*to find*
*in*
*other sources.*

You
have sought love,
now
seek the One
Who is love.

You
have needed healing;
seek the Healer,
the One
Who has been wounded for you,
so that
you can be made whole.

Everything
you need
will be found in God
through
Christ Jesus.

He
is waiting for you
now.

Go to Him.

God
loves to see
His children
prosper.

God's purposes for us
are
honorable
and
for our best interest.

As we go through a trial,
God
is in it with us.

Should we fall,
God
is there to pick us up.

If we have fear,
God
is always there
to
protect us.

We
are greatly blessed
by
being in the family of God.

What an honor
to be called
"His children."

Think of it.

Children
of
the living God.

Part of the family
God
has called as His own.

Seek Him
to really understand
what
that means.

Stand with others
in their time of trouble.
Hold them before the Father
in prayer
in these times
of growth.

I love You, Lord.

You
are the living God
and
I praise Your Name.

All Heaven
is established
to give
You
honor and glory.

Be pleased
with
my life, Lord.

Let it glorify You
in
all that I do.

Change my heart
to desire
only
Your will,
so that
You
may be glorified.

Be exalted, Lord.

Let
Your people
honor You.

Establish Your Name
on our lips
to be presented
to a dying world.

Let us
bring
glory to Your Name
in all we do.

We choose to serve You.

Trust God
to make you what you need to be.

He
is the source
of
all
of our needs.

Is it conceivable
that Jesus
would
take someone
who
does not have
the same motives,
desires
and
loves
as He has
to be
His bride?

Would you
marry someone
who
looks to others
for
fulfillment?

Of course not!

How, then,
can we expect
to continue
to live for ourselves
when
Jesus
lives for others?

How
can we look
to
the things of this world
which make us happy,
when
Jesus was crucified
by
that same spirit?

How
can we hope
to become
"more"
in the eyes of others,
when
Jesus
wants us
to lay our lives down?

To have Jesus
request to have us as His bride,
the Bridegroom
will be looking
for
His completed character
in us.

Nothing else will do.

## Epilogue

After reading all of the previous material, I'm sure that you have a pretty clear picture of the kind of commitment that our Father in Heaven is asking of us. In these last days, it is quite important to have made a full surrender to Jesus, and a determination to follow in His steps. It is, of course, impossible to live as Jesus did in our own strength. It takes a full surrender to God each day, and the invitation for our Lord Jesus to infuse us with inner strength. It is by His power that we have the possibility of walking as Jesus did in a dying world.

*Dear Lord.*
*I realize that it is impossible for me to live*
*the life that You have called me to*
*in my own strength.*

*Jesus, I surrender fully to Your Lordship over my life.*
*I believe that You have been raised from the dead,*
*and*
*are now at work on my behalf.*

*I submit to Your will, Jesus,*
*and*
*call upon You to give me the strength required*
*to walk as You did.*
*You are my Lord,*
*and*
*I choose to follow only You.*

Signed _____ Date _____

Jim and Merry Corbett are in full-time ministry together. They are available for your church service or special event.

Merry is an accomplished pianist and worship leader. Her desire is to provide a platform of music and praise for the Holy Spirit to move as He wishes.

Jim presents the heart of God in a unique fashion, using the Word, stories, and convicting exhortation in preparation for a deeper commitment to Christ, a preparation of the bride.

Jim and Merry Corbett, together with their daughter, Jubilee, desire to be used to reach those who need to know more of their loving Savior. If you have an event that will allow them to do that, you can contact them by writing:

Jim and Merry Corbett
Community Services Network
P.O. Box 1116
Brookfield, Wisconsin 53008-1116
or
E-Mail them at:
stone@worldimpact.com
Fax. 414.369.2912

Available Publications
through
Community Services Network

**"A White Stone"**
**ISBN 0 - 9657268-0-0**
Quite possibly the most life-changing novel of our time
A true call to holiness
Makes the perfect outreach gift

**"A White Stone Workbook"**
**ISBN 0 - 9657268-1-9**
A call to holiness and commitment using the traditional
Jewish wedding of old, and a study of the character of
Jesus as preparation for His coming -
a bridal preparation.

**"From Our Father's Heart To You"**
**ISBN 0 - 9657268-2-7**
Words and exhortations given in prayer that will bring
even the hardest heart to understand our need to draw
close to our Father.

All are available through your local bookstore,
or contact us:
Community Services Network
P.O. Box 1116
Brookfield, Wisconsin 53008-1116
E-Mail stone@worldimpact.com
Fax 414.369.2912

Discounts available to ministries or for multiple sales.

Community Services Network
has a radio program that is available to all stations.

"Amazing Grace,"
the daily 15 minute program
addressing the events of our time
from the perspective of the waiting bride,
brings into focus the season in which we live.

"Amazing Grace,"
with
author Jim Corbett
and
CSN president Ron Plender,
is a comfortable "talk format" program
designed to quiet the worried heart
and stir it to love as Jesus did.

If you can't find
"Amazing Grace"
on your local station,
ask them to carry it.

"Amazing Grace"
is produced by
Community Services Network
P.O. Box 1116
Brookfield, Wisconsin    53008-1116

Phone 414.369.2911
Fax     414.369.2912
E-Mail  stone@worldimpact.com